Cover photo: Pheasant 29

Illustrations by Karen Rolnick

German & Viennese Cooking

Delair

ISBN: 0-8326-0626-X

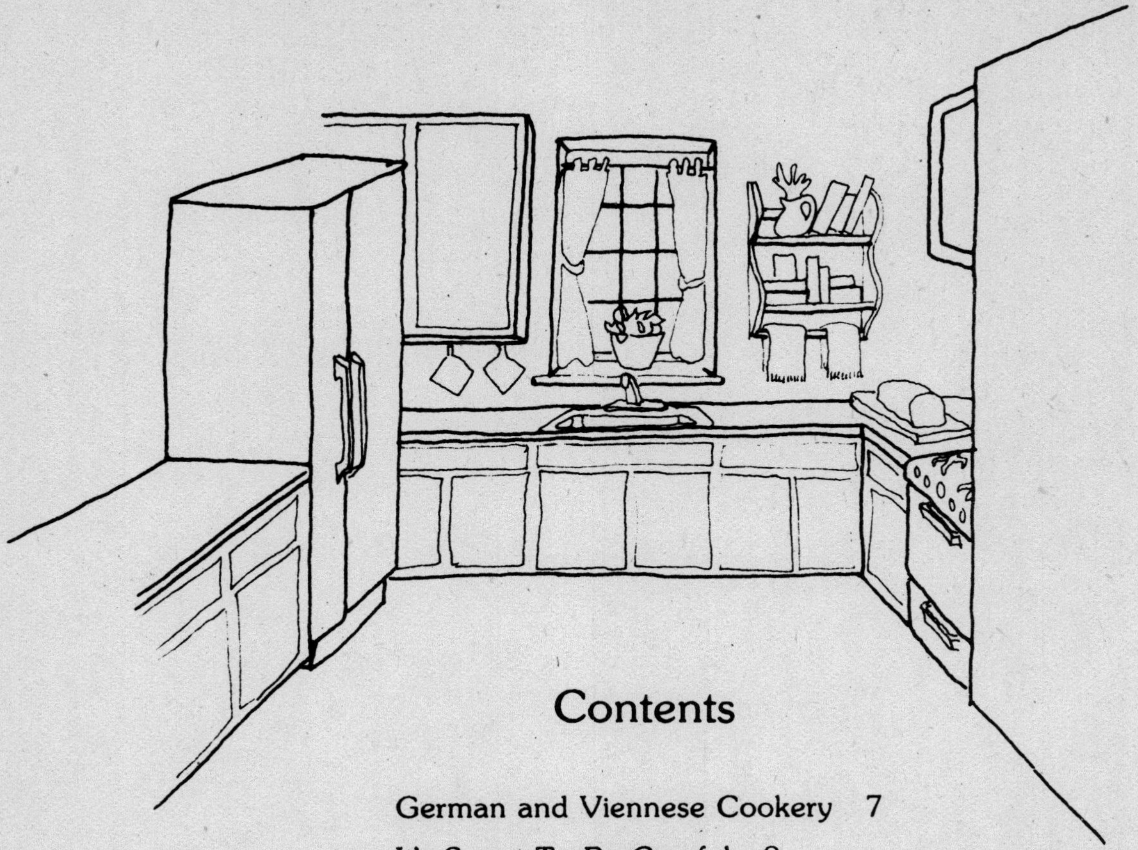

Contents

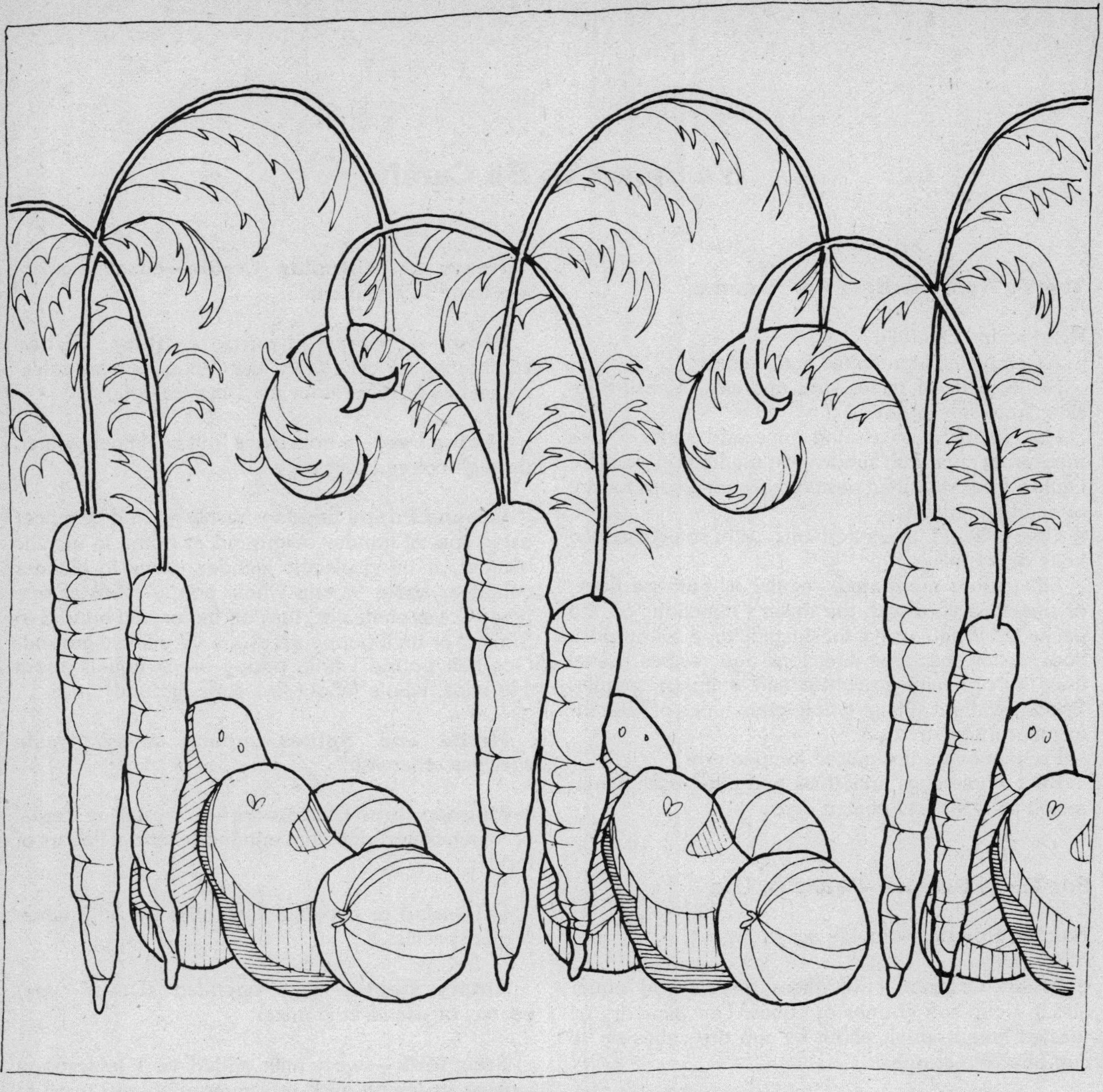

German & Viennese Cookery

Even in the United States, where rapid change is the accepted order of things, German restaurants have a way of going on forever. The waiters are usually venerable, and the patrons look as if they have grown up on the premises and found a happy second home there. There is a hearty, substantial, enduring and endearing atmosphere, congenial to young and old, and comfortable as the family hearth. German cooking and its Viennese first cousin may be described in almost the same words. Both are generous, hearty, comfortable, taste worderful, smell wonderful, and are wonderfully staying.

The basic traditions of German cookery developed in the aromatic kitchens of Hausfrauen who resisted the influence of France and Italy and borrowed ideas only from their Central European neighbors. Viennese cooking, coming into full flower in a city that was for many years the crossroads of Europe, reflects the influence of many nations.

When we think of German and Viennese cooking we are apt to recall them with our noses—the redolent fragrance of sweet-sour is characteristic of the Central European tradition and one of its great gifts—excellent soups, zestful sausages, delicious coffee cakes and breads, meltingly delectable strudel, apple pancakes that are almost as big as cartwheels, and dumplings. Dumplings in overwhelming variety are one of the true glories of Central European cooking and a boon to the eating pleasure of the world.

It's Smart To Be Careful

There's No Substitute For Accuracy

Read recipe carefully

Assemble all ingredients and utensils.

Select pans of paper kind and size. Measure inside, from rim to rim.

Use standard measuring cups and spoons. Use measuring cups with subdivision marked on sides for liquids. Use graduated nested measuring cups for dry or solid ingredients.

Check liquid measurements with straight-edged knife or spatula.

Sift (before measuring) regular all-purpose flour, or not, in accord with the miller's directions on the package. When using the instant type all-purpose flour, follow package directions and recipes. Level flour in cup with straight-edged knife or spatula. Spoon, without sifting, whole-grain types of flour into measuring cup.

Preheat oven at required temperature.

Beat whole eggs until thick and piled softly when recipe calls for well-beaten eggs.

For These Recipes—What To Use

Baking Powder—double action type.

Bread Crumbs—two slices fresh bread equal about 1 cup soft crumbs or cubes. One slice dry or toasted bread equals about ½ cup dry cubes or ¼ cup fine, dry crumbs.

Buttered Crumbs—soft or dry bread or cracker crumbs tossed in melted butter. Use 1 to 2 tablespoons butter for 1 cup soft crumbs and 2 to 4 tablespoons butter for 1 cup dry crumbs.

Chocolate—unsweetened chocolate. A substitution for 1 sq. (1 oz.) chocolate is 3 to 4 tablespoons cocoa plus 1 tablespoon shortening.

Chocolate (no melt)—1-oz. packets or envelopes chocolate-flavored product or ingredient.

Cornstarch—thickening agent having double the thickening power of flour.

Cream—light, table or coffee cream containing 18% to 20% butterfat.

Heavy or Whipping Cream—containing not less than 30% butterfat.

Flour—regular all-purpose flour. When substituting for cake flour, use 1 cup minus 2 tablespoons all-purpose flour for 1 cup cake flour.

Grated Peel—whole citrus fruit peel finely grated through colored part only.

Ground Poppy Seeds—freshly ground by grocer using special grinder or ground at home in electric blender. If using electric blender, place in blender container about ½ cup whole poppy seeds at one time. Cover container, turn on motor and grind 3 to 5 min., or until poppy seeds are very finely ground. One-half pound whole poppy seeds equals about 1⅔ cups, whole (about 2½ cups, ground).

Herbs and Spices—ground unless recipe specifies otherwise.

Monosodium Glutamate—a crystalline cereal or vegetable product that enhances natural flavors of foods.

Oil—salad or cooking. Use olive oil only when recipe specifies it.

Rotary Beater—hand-operated (Dover type) beater, or use electric mixer.

Sour Milk—sweet milk added to 1 tablespoon vinegar or lemon juice in a measuring cup to fill to 1-cup line; stir. Or use buttermilk.

Sugar—granulated (beet or cane).

Vinegar—cider vinegar unless otherwise specified.

How To Do It

Baste—spoon liquid over cooking food to add moisture and flavor; or use baster.

Blanch Nuts—the flavor and crisp texture of nuts are best maintained when nuts are allowed to remain in water the shortest possible time during blanching.

Therefore, blanch only about ½ cup at a time; repeat as many times as necessary for larger amounts. Bring to rapid boil enough water to cover shelled nuts. Drop in nuts. Turn off heat and allow nuts to remain in the water about 1 min.; drain, or remove with fork or slotted spoon. Place between folds of absorbent paper; pat dry. Squeeze nuts between thumb and fingers to remove skins or peel. Place on dry absorbent paper. To dry thoroughly, frequently shift nuts to dry spots on paper.

Grate Nuts—use a rotary type grater with hand-operating crank. Follow manufacturer's directions. Grated nuts should be fine and light; do not use an electric blender for grating or grinding nuts called for in these recipes.

Toast Nuts—put blanched nuts in a shallow baking pan. Heat nuts (plain or brushed lightly with cooking oil) in 350°F oven until delicately browned. Move and turn occasionally with spoon. Or add blanched nuts to a heavy skillet in which butter (about 1 tablespoon per cup of nuts) has been melted; or use oil. Brown nuts lightly, moving and turning constantly, over moderate heat.

Salt Nuts—toast nuts; drain on absorbent paper and sprinkle with salt.

Boil—cook in liquid in which bubbles rise continually and break on the surface. Boiling temperature of water at sea level is 212°F.

Clean Celery—trim roots and cut off leaves. Leaves may be used for added flavor in soups and stuffings; leaves may be left on inner stalks when used as relish. Separate stalks, remove blemishes and wash. Proceed as directed in recipe.

Clean Garlic—separate into cloves and remove thin, papery outer skin.

Clean Green Pepper—rinse and slice away from pod and stem; trim off any white membrane; rinse away seeds; cut into strips, dice or prepare as directed in recipes.

Clean and Slice Mushrooms—wipe with a clean, damp cloth and cut off tips of stems; slice lengthwise through stems and caps.

Clean Onions (dry)—cut off root end and thin slice from stem end; peel and rinse.

Cut Dried Fruits (uncooked) or Marshmallows—cut with scissors dipped frequently in water.

Dice—cut into small cubes.

Flake Fish—with a fork separate canned (cooked) fish into flakes (thin, layer-like pieces). Remove bony tissue from crab meat; salmon bones are edible.

Fold—use flexible spatula and slip it down side of bowl to bottom. Turn bowl quarter turn. Lift spatula through mixture along side of bowl with blade parallel to surface of material. Cut down and under; turn bowl and repeat process until material seems blended. With every fourth stroke, bring spatula up through center.

Hard-Cook Eggs—put eggs into large saucepan and cover completely with cold or warm water. Cover. Bring water rapidly to just boiling. Turn off heat immediately. If necessary to prevent further boiling, remove pan from heat source. Let stand covered 20 to 22 min. Plunge eggs promptly into running cold water. Crack shell under water and roll between hands to loosen. When cooled, start peeling at large end.

Marinate—allow food to stand in liquid (usually an oil and acid mixture) to impart additional flavor.

Measure Brown Sugar—pack so firmly into dry measuring cup that sugar will hold shape of cup when turned out.

Measure Granulated Brown Sugar—see substitution table on package before pouring into measuring cup.

Melt Chocolate—unsweetened, over simmering water; sweet or semi-sweet, over hot (not simmering) water.

Mince—cut or chop into small, fine pieces.

Panbroil Bacon—place in cold skillet only as many bacon slices as will lie flat. Cook slowly, turning frequently. Pour off fat as it collects. When bacon is evenly crisped and browned, remove from skillet and drain on absorbent paper.

Prepare Quick Broth—dissolve in 1 cup hot water, 1 chicken bouillon cube for chicken broth, or 1 beef bouillon cube for meat broth.

Rice—force through ricer, sieve, or food mill.

Scald Milk—heat in top of double boiler over simmering water or in a heavy saucepan over direct heat just until a thin film appears.

Sieve—force through coarse sieve or food mill.

Simmer—cook in liquid just below boiling point; bubbles form slowly and break below surface.

Unmold Gelatin—run tip of knife around top edge of mold to loosen. Invert mold onto chilled plate. If necessary, wet a clean towel in hot water and wring it almost dry. Wrap hot towel around mold for a few seconds only. (If mold does not loosen, repeat.)

Water Bath (Hot)—set a baking pan on oven rack and place the filled baking dish in pan. Surround with very hot water to at least 1-in. depth.

When You Broil

Set temperature control of range at Broil. Distance from top of food to source of heat determines intensity of heat upon food.

When You Deep Fry

About 20 min. before ready to deep fry, fill a deep saucepan one-half to two-thirds full with hydrogenated vegetable shortening, all-purpose shortening, lard or cooking oil. Heat fat slowly to temperature given in the recipe. A deep-frying thermometer is an accurate guide for deep-frying.

If thermometer is not available, the following bread cube method may be used as a guide: A 1-in. cube of bread browns in 60 seconds at 350°F to 375°F.

When using an automatic deep-fryer, follow manufacturer's directions for amount of fat.

Oven Temperatures

Very Slow	250°F to 275°F
Slow	300°F to 325°F
Moderate	350°F to 375°F
Hot	400°F to 425°F
Very Hot	450°F to 475°F
Extreme Hot	500°F to 525°F

Use a portable oven thermometer to double-check oven temperature.

A Check-List for Successful Baking

✓ **Read Again** "It's Smart To Be Careful—There's No Substitute for Accuracy."

✓ **Place Oven Rack** so top of product will be almost at center of oven. Stagger pans so no pan is directly over another and they do not touch each other or walls of oven. Place single pan so that center of product is as near center of oven as possible.

✓ **Prepare Pan**—For cakes with shortening and for tortes, grease bottom of pan only; line with waxed paper; grease the waxed paper. If cake (plain or frosted) is to be cut and stored in pan, omit waxed paper. For cakes without shortening (sponge type), do not grease or line pan. For most yeast breads and quick breads, grease sheet. For cookies, lightly grease cookie sheets. If recipe directs "set out pan," do not grease or line pan.

✓ **Have All Ingredients** at room temperature unless recipe specifies otherwise.

✓ **Sift** (before measuring) regular all-purpose flour, or not, in accord with the miller's directions on the package. When using the instant type all-purpose flour, follow package directions and recipes. Level flour in cup with straight-edged knife or spatula. Spoon, without sifting, whole-grain types of flour into measuring cup.

✓ **Cream Butter** (alone or with flavorings) by stirring, rubbing or beating with spoon or electric mixer until softened. Add sugar in small amounts, creaming thoroughly after each addition. Thorough creaming helps to insure a fine-grained cake.

✓ **Beat Whole Eggs** until thick and piled softly when recipe calls for well-beaten eggs.

✓ **Beat Egg Whites** as follows: Frothy—entire mass forms bubbles; Rounded peaks—peaks turn over slightly when beater is slowly lifted upright; Stiff peaks—remain standing when beater is slowly lifted upright.

✓ **When Liquid And Dry Ingredients** are added to batters, add alternately, beginning and ending with dry. Add dry ingredients in fourths, liquid in thirds. After each addition, beat only until smooth. Finally, beat only until batter is smooth (do not overbeat). Scrape spoon or beater and bottom and sides of bowl during mixing.

If using an electric mixer, beat mixture at a low speed when alternately adding liquid and dry ingredients.

✓ **Fill Cake Pans** one-half to two-thirds full.

✓ **Tap Bottom Of Cake Pan** sharply with hand or on table to release air bubbles before placing in oven.

✓ **Apply Baking Tests** when minimum baking time is up. For cakes or tortes, touch lightly at center; if it springs back, cake is done. Or insert a cake tester, or wooden pick in center; if it comes out clean, cake is done.

✓ **Cool Butter Cakes** 10 min., tortes 15 min., in pan on cooling rack after removing from oven; or cool as recipe directs.

✓ **Remove Cake Or Torte** from pan after cooling. Run spatula gently around inside of pan. Cover with cooling rack. Invert and remove pan. Turn right side up immediately after peeling off waxed paper. Or remove from pan as recipe directs. Cool cake or torte completely before frosting.

✓ **Fill Layer Cakes Or Tortes**—Spread filling or frosting over top of bottom layer. Cover with the second layer. Repeat procedure if more layers are used. If necessary, hold layers in position with wooden picks; remove when filling is set.

✓ **Frost Filled Layer Cakes Or Tortes**—Frost sides first, working rapidly. See that frosting touches plate all around bottom, leaving no gaps. Pile remaining frosting on top of cake and spread lightly.

✓ **Test** for lukewarm liquid (80°F to 85°F) by placing a drop on wrist; it will feel neither hot nor cold.

✓ **Knead Dough** by folding opposite side over toward you. Using heels of hands, gently push dough away. Give it one-quarter turn. Repeat process rhythmically until the dough is smooth and elastic, 5 to 8 min., using as little additional flour as possible. Always turn the dough in the same direction.

✓ **Remove Rolls, Bread and Cookies** from pans as they come from the oven, unless otherwise directed. Set on cooling racks to cool.

✓ **Keep Tops** of yeast loaves and rolls soft by immediately brushing with butter as they come from the oven.

Soups

Soup is an important part of the daily menu of Central Europe. Germans and Austrians are hearty eaters and many of their soups are made to match their appetites. Small dumplings, noodles, rice, lentils, and many ingenious flour and egg mixtures (such as Riebele, Fladle and Butterbiskuit) are commonly used to give substance and interest to soups. Vegetable soups are usually creamed or thickened with roux. In some parts of Germany fruit soups are popular, and they are usually served warm. Soup accompaniments such as Custard Cubes are flavorful tidbits with which the German Hausfrau adds eye appeal, flavor and extra heartiness to the clear soups she serves to her family.

Vienna "Peas"

- **3/4 cup sifted all-purpose flour**
- **1/4 teaspoon salt**
- **1 egg**
- **2 tablespoons milk**

1. Set out a deep saucepan or automatic deep-fryer and heat fat to 375°F.
2. Sift flour and salt together into a bowl. Make a well in center and set aside.
3. Beat egg and milk together. Add all at one time to the dry ingredients. Beat until well blended and smooth.
4. Drop batter by 1/4 teaspoonfuls into the hot fat. Deep-fry only as many balls at one time as will float uncrowded one layer deep. Fry 1 to 2 min., or until balls are golden brown. Lift from fat with slotted spoon, drain over fat a few seconds, remove to absorbent paper.
5. Float some of the "peas" in each plate of clear soup.

About 2 cups "peas"

Green Pea Soup with Sour Cream

- **6 cups Quick Meat Broth (page 9)**
- **2 lbs. fresh peas**
- **¼ cup butter**
- **¼ cup all-purpose flour**
- **½ teaspoon salt**
- **⅛ teaspoon white pepper**
- **1 egg yolk**
- **½ cup thick sour cream**
- **1 tablespoon chopped parsley**
- **Strips of smoked tongue**

1. Prepare Quick Meat Broth in a large heavy saucepan or sauce pot.
2. To retain their delicate flavor, rinse and shell peas just before using. Cook the peas in the broth about 20 min., or until tender. Remove and reserve 1 cup of the broth. Set peas aside.
3. Meanwhile, heat butter in a saucepan, and blend in flour, salt, and white pepper. Heat until mixture bubbles. Remove from heat. Add gradually, stirring in, the cup of reserved broth.
4. Pour mixture gradually into the pea soup, stirring constantly. Bring to boiling. Cook 1 to 2 min.
5. Beat egg yolk slightly. Quickly stir about 3 tablespoons of the hot soup into the egg yolk. Immediately return egg-yolk mixture to soup, stirring vigorously.
6. Reduce heat and cook soup until thoroughly heated, about 5 min., stirring constantly. Do not boil. Remove from heat and force through a sieve. Return to the saucepan.
7. Stirring vigorously with a French whip, whisk beater, or fork, add sour cream in very small amounts and stir in parsley.
8. Cook soup over low heat, stirring constantly, 3 to 5 min., until well heated; do not boil. Serve soup garnished with strips of smoked tongue.

About 3 pts. soup

Lentil Soup with Frankfurters

- **2 qts. Quick Meat Broth (page 9)**
- **1½ cups (about ½ lb.) lentils**
- **1 ham bone, cracked**
- **2 stalks celery, sliced**
- **2 carrots, washed, pared or scraped and sliced**
- **1 teaspoon salt**
- **¼ teaspoon pepper**
- **3 sprigs chervil or parsley**
- **2 tablespoons butter**
- **2 medium-size onions, thinly sliced**
- **6 frankfurters, cut diagonally into ½-in. slices**

1. Prepare Quick Meat Broth in a sauce pot or kettle having a tight-fitting cover.
2. Rinse, sort and add to sauce pot lentils and ham bone. Cover sauce pot and bring slowly to boiling.
3. Meanwhile, prepare celery and carrots.
4. Skim foam from broth; add the vegetables with salt, pepper and chervil or parsley. Cover and bring to boiling; reduce heat and simmer 2 hrs., or until lentils are tender and soft enough to mash easily. Remove from heat and remove ham bone. Force soup mixture through a coarse sieve or food mill and return to sauce pot. Set aside.
5. Heat butter in a skillet. Add onions and frankfurters and cook over medium heat, occasionally moving and turning with a spoon. Cook until the onions are tender and frankfurters slices are lightly browned.
6. Add the onions and frankfurter slices to the soup. Heat soup about 10 min., or until very hot.

About 2 qts. soup

Vegetable Soup

- **1 soup bone, cracked**
- **3 qts. cold water**
- **1 tablespoon salt**
- **1 lb. potatoes, (3 medium-size), washed, pared and diced**
- **1 lb. green beans, washed, ends cut off and beans cut into halves**
- **3 small carrots, washed, pared or scraped, and cut into quarters lengthwise**
- **2 medium-size onions, chopped (about 1 cup)**
- **2 stalks celery, cut into ½-in. pieces**
- **2 tablespoons minced parsley**
- **2 tablespoons sugar**
- **2 teaspoons salt**
- **2 28-oz. cans tomatoes (about 6 cups, sieved)**
- **2 tablespoons shortening**
- **¼ cup flour**
- **¼ cup all-purpose flour**

1. Put soup bone into a large sauce pot or kettle having a cover, with water and salt. Cover and bring to boiling, reduce heat and simmer 1½ hrs. During cooking, occasionally remove foam that forms on top.
2. Meanwhile prepare potatoes, green beans, carrots, onions, celery and parsley.
3. After 1½ hrs., add vegetables to soup with sugar and salt. Simmer 30 min., or until vegetables are tender.
4. Just before vegetables are tender, force tomatoes through a sieve or food mill. Set aside.
5. Heat shortening in a saucepan. Blend in ¼ cup flour.
6. Add ¼ cup all-purpose flour and cook over low heat, stirring constantly. Cook until mixture bubbles and is lightly browned. Remove from heat and add gradually, stirring constantly, 1 cup of the soup stock. Cook 1 to 2 min., or until smooth. Blend into soup with the sieved tomatoes. Bring to boiling, reduce heat and simmer 5 to 10 min., or until soup is slightly thickened. Remove soup bone. Serve steaming hot.

8 to 10 servings

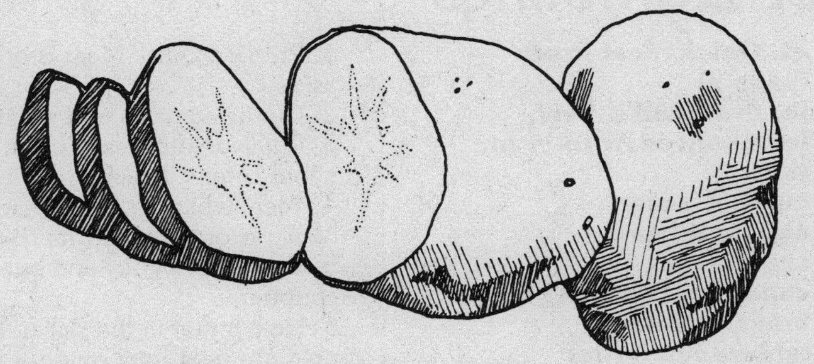

Potato Soup

- **6 medium-size (about 2 lbs.) potatoes**
- **5 cups cold water**
- **1 carrot, washed, pared or scraped, and cut into pieces**
- **1 leek, washed thoroughly and thinly sliced (white part only)**
- **1 stalk celery, cut into pieces**
- **1 medium-size onion cut into slices**
- **2 teaspoons salt**
- **¼ teaspoon white pepper**
- **¼ teaspoon thyme**
- **¼ teaspoon marjoram**
- **1 bay leaf**
- **1 beef bouillon cube**
- **2 tablespoons butter**
- **3 tablespoons all-purpose flour**
- **Finely chopped parsley**

1. Set out a heavy 3-qt. saucepan or sauce pot having a tight-fitting cover.
2. Wash, pare and cut potatoes into ¼-in. slices. Put into the saucepan or sauce pot with water.
3. Cover and bring to boiling. Reduce heat to medium and add carrot, leek, celery, onion, salt, pepper, thyme, marjoram and bay leaf.
4. Cover and cook about 1 hr., or until vegetables are tender.
5. Remove the carrot, leek, celery, onion and bay leaf with a slotted spoon and discard.
6. Remove 1 cup of the potato broth; add bouillon cube to it. Force remaining potato mixture through a fine sieve into a saucepan.
7. Heat butter over low heat. Blend in flour. Heat until mixture bubbles. Stir the 1 cup of potato broth and gradually add to the butter-flour mixture, stirring constantly. Pour into the soup and blend well. Return to heat; bring to boiling. Reduce heat and simmer gently 5 to 10 min., or until soup is thoroughly heated. Garnish with parsley.

About 2½ pts. soup

Custard Cubes

- **1/3 cup milk**
- **1 egg**
- **1/8 teaspoon salt**
- **1/8 teaspoon paprika**
- **Few grains pepper**

1. Heat water for hot water bath.
2. Scald milk.
3. Beat egg, salt, paprika and pepper together slightly.
4. Pour scalded milk slowly into the egg mixture, beating constantly. Strain the custard into a shallow baking pan (about 5 in. square).
5. Bake in the hot water bath at 325°F about 30 min., or until a silver knife inserted halfway between center and edge comes out clean. Cool. Cut custard into 1/2-in. cubes or fancy shapes and slip into hot soup just before serving.

About 100 1/2-in cubes

Liver Dumplings

- **1 qt. Quick Meat Broth (page 9)**
- **1/2 lb. liver (calf's, beef, lamb),sliced 1/4 to 1/2 in. thick**
- **1 cup hot water**
- **1 egg, well beaten**
- **1/3 cup cream**
- **3 cups (4 to 5 slices) soft bread crumbs**
- **1 tablespoon butter**
- **3 tablespoons finely chopped onion**
- **1 clove garlic, minced**
- **1 teaspoon finely chopped parsley**
- **1/2 teaspoon salt**
- **1/4 teaspoon marjoram**

1. Prepare Quick Meat Broth in a large, heavy saucepan and set aside.
2. Cut away tubes and outer membrane, if necessary from liver.
3. Put liver into a skillet with hot water. Cover skillet and simmer about 5 min. Drain.
4. Meanwhile, put egg, cream, and soft bread crumbs into a bowl, in order, and mix. Set aside.
5. Cool liver slightly and put through the medium blade of a food chopper.
6. Heat butter in the skillet. Add onion and garlic and cook over medium heat until onion is tender.
7. Add liver and contents of skillet to the bread crumb mixture with parsley, salt and marjoram. Shape liver mixture into balls about 3/4 in. in diameter.
8. Bring the meat broth to boiling. Drop dumplings into the broth. Cook only as many dumplings (about 12) as will lie uncrowded one layer deep. Cook 3 to 5 min., or until dumplings rise to surface of broth. Remove dumplings with a slotted spoon and drain over broth a few seconds. Keep warm while cooking remaining dumplings. Use several dumplings for each serving of clear soup.

About 2 doz. dumplings

Breads

Connoisseurs everywhere pay honor to the superb coffee cakes of Austria and Germany. Rich enough to be eaten as desserts, often bursting with candied fruit or flavored with almond, poppy or caraway seeds or ground nuts, these wonderful, hearty breads are famous far beyond the countries of their origin.

Almond-Crumb Coffee Cake

- **¼ cup (about 1½ oz.) almonds**
- **Filled Berlin Doughnuts (Bismarcks, page 23; decrease milk to ½ cup, substitute 1 teaspoon grated lemon peel for the orange juice and omit rum extract)**
- **½ cup sifted all-purpose flour**
- **3 tablespoons sugar**
- **1 teaspoon cinnamon**
- **½ teaspoon grated lemon peel**
- **4 tablespoons firm butter**
- **Melted butter**

1. Blanch and set almonds aside.
2. Prepare dough for Filled Berlin Doughnuts. After the dough has doubled and just before turning dough onto floured surface, lightly grease the bottoms 2 8-in. round layer cake pans.
3. Divide dough into two balls and pat out each in a greased pan. Dough should be ¼ to ½ in. thick. Cover with waxed paper and a towel and let rise 30 to 45 min., or until dough is doubled.
4. For Streusel topping—Meanwhile, finely chop the blanched almonds. Blend in flour, sugar, cinnamon and lemon peel. Cut in butter with a pastry blender or two knives until mixture is size of small peas.
5. When dough has doubled, brush tops with melted butter. Sprinkle dough evenly with the almond-flour mixture.
6. Bake at 350°F 35 to 40 min., or until coffee cake tests done.

2 8-in. round coffee cakes

Quick Crumb Coffee Cake: Follow recipe for Almond-Crumb Coffee Cake. Omit almonds. For the Streusel Topping, omit nuts and lemon peel and, if desired, also omit cinnamon.

Apple Crumb Coffee Cake: Follow recipe for Almond-Crumb Coffee Cake. After first rising, divide dough into four balls instead of two. Pat out only one ball in each pan and set two balls aside. Lightly brush dough in pans with melted butter. Wash, quarter, pare and cut into thin slices 3 medium-size **apples.** Arrange apple slices over the dough in each pan. Lightly brush apple slices with **melted butter.** Sprinkle with a mixture of 1/3 cup **sugar** and 2 teaspoons **cinnamon.** Pat out remaining two balls of dough and carefully arrange over the apples. Proceed as in recipe.

Basic Yeast Dough

- **2 cups milk**
- **2 pkgs. active dry yeast**
- **½ cup warm water, 110°F to 115°F (Or if using compressed yeast, soften 2 cakes in ½ cup lukewarm water, 80°F to 85°F)**
- **1 cup butter, softened**
- **½ cup sugar**
- **2 teaspoons salt**
- **2 teaspoons grated lemon peel**
- **10 cups sifted all-purpose flour**
- **4 eggs, well beaten**

1. Scald milk. Meanwhile, soften yeast in water. Set aside.
2. Meanwhile, put butter, sugar, salt, and lemon peel into a large bowl.
3. Immediately pour scalded milk over ingredients in bowl and stir mixture until butter is completely melted. When mixture has cooled to lukewarm, blend in 2 cups of flour, beating until smooth. Stir softened yeast and add, mixing well.
4. Measure 7 or 8 cups of flour. Add about one-half of the flour to the dough and beat until very smooth.
5. Add in thirds, beating well after each addition, eggs, well beaten. Then beat in enough of the remaining flour to make a soft dough. Turn dough onto a lightly floured surface and allow it to rest 5 to 10 min.
6. Knead dough. Form dough into a large smooth ball and place it in a lightly greased, deep bowl. Turn dough to bring greased surface to top*. Cover with waxed paper and towel; let stand in warm place (about 80°F) until dough is doubled (about 1½ hrs.)
7. Punch down dough with fist and turn out onto a lightly floured surface. Allow dough to rest 10 min. before shaping.
8. Complete as directed in any of the following variations.

Enough dough for 4 coffee cakes or 4 doz. rolls

*This dough may be kept about 3 days in the refrigerator. Make sure dough is greased and well-covered to keep surface of dough moist and elastic. Punch down dough occasionally as it rises. Remove amount of dough needed for a single baking and immediately return remainder to refrigerator. Proceed as directed in the desired variation.

Note: For bread, shape dough into 3 loaves. Place in 9½x5¼x2¾-in. loaf pans, lightly greased. When dough is light, bake at 400°F about 50 min.

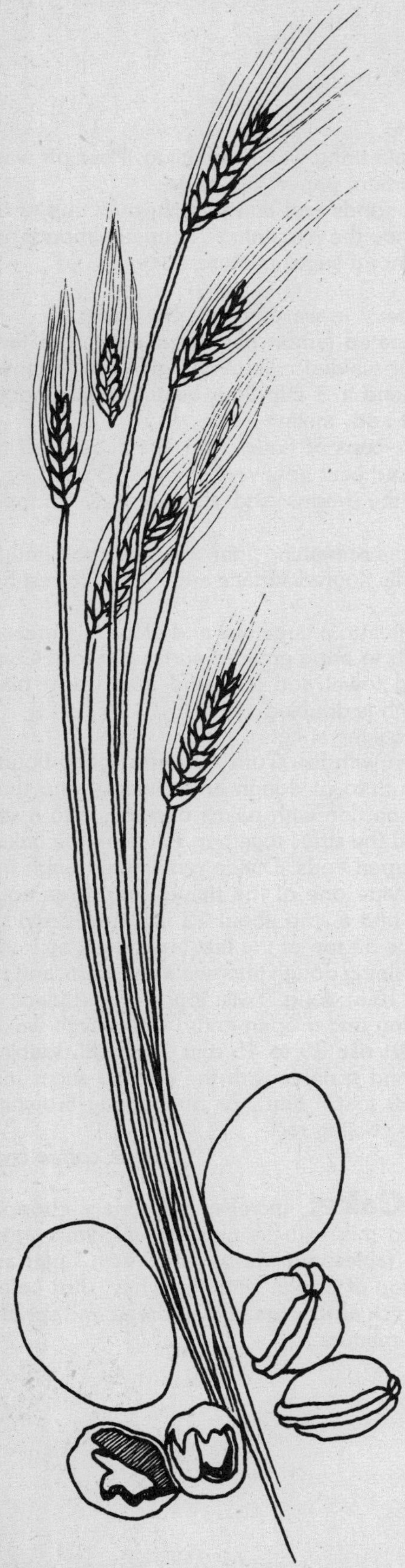

Sweet Rolls: To prepare 2 doz. rolls, use one-half of dough in recipe for Basic Yeast Dough. Butter two 11x7x1½-in. pans. Roll dough ½ in. thick. Using a sharp knife, cut dough into twenty-four 3x2-in. rectangles. Spread rectangles almost to edges with fruit preserves. Starting with the shorter side, roll up rectangles of dough. Arrange twelve rolls in each pan. Brush generously with melted **butter.** Cover with waxed paper and a towel and let rise in a warm place (80°F) until almost doubled.

1. Bake at 350°F 25 to 30 min., or until rolls are lightly browned.
2. Meanwhile, prepare a glaze by thoroughly blending together **confectioners' sugar** and **milk** or **cream.** Remove rolls from pans to cooling racks; cool slightly. Using a spoon, drizzle glaze over rolls.

Plum Coffee Cake: To prepare 2 rich coffee cakes, decrease ingredients to ½ amounts in recipe for Basic Yeast Dough except decrease milk from 2 cups to ¼ cup, salt from 2 teaspoons to ½ teaspoon, and flour from 10 cups to 3 cups. Proceed as directed. Lightly grease two 9-in. round layer cake pans (bottoms only). Rinse and remove pits from 25 (about 1¼ lbs.) small **Italian plums.** Divide dough into halves; press evenly into pans. Brush with **melted butter.** Arrange plums cut side up on dough to 1 in. from edge of pan. Sprinkle with a mixture of about 1½ cups **sugar** (depending on tartness of fruit) 2 tablespoons **flour** and 2 teaspoons **cinnamon.** Dot with ¼ cup **butter.** Cover with waxed paper and a towel and let rise in a warm place (80°F) until almost doubled, about 1 hr. Bake at 375°F 15 min. Then pour a mixture of 4 **egg yolks,** beaten, 2 tablespoons **sugar,** and ¼ cup **cream** over plums. Continue baking 15 to 20 min., or until custard topping is set.

Cinnamon Coffee Cake: To prepare 2 coffee cakes, use one-half of dough in recipe for Basic Yeast Dough. Lightly grease the bottoms of two 11x7x1½-in. pans or two 10-in. round layer cake pans. Divide dough into halves and roll out to fit the pans. Fit into pans. Brush dough with ¼ cup melted **butter;** sprinkle with a mixture of ⅔ cup **sugar** and 2 teaspoons **cinnamon.** Cover with waxed paper and a towel and let rise in a warm place (80°F) until almost doubled. Bake at 375°F about 20 min.

Crumb Coffee Cake: Follow recipe for Cinnamon Coffee Cake; omit sugar-cinnamon mixture. Prepare and top with **Streusel Topping** (see Quick Crumb Coffee Cake, page 18).

Apple Coffee Cake: Follow recipe for Plum Coffee Cake; substitute 2 medium-size firm **cooking apples** for Italian plums. Wash, quarter, core, pare and slice the apples; arrange on dough. Reduce cinnamon to 1 teaspoon; add ¼ teaspoon *each* **nutmeg** and **cloves.** Omit egg-cream mixture. Bake 35 min. Any desired fresh fruit, such as **cherries** or **peaches,** may be substituted for the apples. The amount of sugar sprinkled over fruit will vary with the tartness of the fruit.

Coffee Braid

1½ cups water
1 cup (about 5 oz.) dark seedless raisins
1 cup (about 5 oz.) blanched almonds
2 tablespoons sugar
1 cup milk
1 pkg. active dry yeast
¼ cup warm water, 110°F to 115°F (Or if using compressed yeast, soften 1 cake in ¼ cup lukewarm water, 80°F to 85°F.)
⅔ cup sugar
½ cup butter, softened
1 teaspoon grated lemon peel
1 teaspoon salt
4½ cups sifted all-purpose flour
2 eggs, well beaten
Egg white, slightly beaten

A baking sheet will be needed.

1. Bring water to boiling.
2. Add raisins, and again bring water to boiling. Pour off water and drain fruit on absorbent paper. Set aside.
3. Set out blanched almonds and coarsely chop ¾ cup of the almonds. Very finely chop the remaining ¼ cup of almonds and mix with sugar. Set almond-sugar mixture aside.
4. Scald milk.
5. Meanwhile, soften yeast in warm water. Set aside.
6. Put sugar, butter, grated lemon peel, and salt into a large bowl. Immediately pour scalded milk over ingredients in bowl.
7. When lukewarm, blend in 1 cup flour beating until smooth. Stir softened yeast and add, mixing well.
8. Measure 3½ to 4½ cups of flour. Add about one-half the flour to yeast mixture and beat until very smooth. Beat in eggs.
9. Add and mix in the raisins and the coarsely chopped almonds.
10. Beat in enough of the remaining flour to make a soft dough. Turn dough onto a lightly floured surface and allow it to rest 5 to 10 min.
11. Knead. Form dough into a large ball and place in a greased deep bowl. Turn dough to bring greased surface to top. Cover with waxed paper and towel and let stand in a warm place (about 80°F) until dough is doubled.
12. Lightly grease the baking sheet.
13. Punch dough down with fist. Turn out onto lightly floured surface. Break off one third of dough and divide it into three equal parts. Roll each portion with palms of hands into a strip about 14 in. long. Braid the strips together. Place on the baking sheet and tuck under open ends. Divide remaining dough into two equal portions. Divide one of the halves into three equal portions and roll each into a strip about 12 in. long. Braid the strips together and place on top of the first braid, tucking under open ends. Divide remaining dough into two equal parts and roll each into a strip about 10 in. long. Twist together and place on top of the braids, tucking under open ends. Cover with waxed paper and towel and let rise 30 to 45 min., or until doubled. Brush with egg white and sprinkle with the almond-sugar mixture. Bake at 350°F 50 to 60 min., or until lightly browned. Remove coffee cake to cooling rack.

1 large coffee braid

Anise Coffee Cake: Increase the finely chopped almonds to ⅓ cup and mix with ¼ cup **sugar.** Omit grated lemon peel and add 1 tablespoon **anise seed** with sugar and butter. Omit brushing top of dough with egg white. Just before baking spread ⅓ cup thick **sour cream** over bread and sprinkle with the almond-sugar mixture.

Nut Snails

2 cups (about 7½ oz.) small pecan halves
1 cup milk or cream
1 pkg. active dry yeast
¼ cup warm water, 110°F to 115°F (Or if using compressed yeast, soften 1 cake in ¼ cup lukewarm water, 80°F to 85°F.)
½ cup sugar
1 teaspoon salt
5 cup sifted all-purpose flour
2 eggs, well beaten
½ cup butter, softened
⅔ cup butter
1 cup firmly packed brown sugar
¼ cup currants
1 tablespoon cinnamon

Twenty-four 2½ in. muffin-pan wells will be needed.

1. Set out small pecan halves. Coarsely chop 1 cup of the pecans, and set them all aside.
2. Scald milk or cream.
3. Meanwhile, soften 1 pkg. active dry yeast in water. Set aside.
4. Meanwhile, put ½ cup of sugar and salt into a large bowl.
5. Pour scalded milk over ingredients in bowl.
6. When mixture is lukewarm and sugar is dissolved, stir mixture and blend in, 1 cup of flour, beating until smooth.
7. Stir softened yeast and add, mixing well.
8. Measure 4 cups of flour and add about one-half of the flour to yeast mixture and beat until very smooth. Beat in eggs.
9. Vigorously beat in ½ cup butter, 2 to 3 tablespoons at a time.
10. Beat in enough remaining flour to make a soft dough. Turn dough onto a lightly floured surface. Let stand 5 to 10 min.
11. Knead. Form dough into a large ball; place it in a greased deep bowl. Turn dough to bring greased surface to top. Cover with waxed paper and towel and let stand in warm place (about 80°F), until doubled.
12. Punch down with fist; pull edges of dough in to center and turn completely over in bowl. Cover with waxed paper and towel and let rise again until nearly doubled.
13. Lightly grease muffin-pan wells.
14. Meanwhile, melt ⅔ cup of butter and put about 1 teaspoon of melted butter in bottom of each muffin-pan well. Reserve remaining butter for Schnecken.
15. Mix sugar, currants, and cinnamon together with chopped nuts.
16. Sprinkle 2 teaspoons of this mixture over butter in each muffin-pan well. Gently press 3 or 4 pecan halves onto mixture in each well.
17. Again punch down dough and form it into two balls. Roll each ball on lightly floured surface into a rectangle ¼ to ⅓ in. thick, 6 to 8 in. wide and 12 in. long. Brush top surface of dough with remaining melted butter and sprinkle evenly with remainder of brown-sugar mixture. Beginning with longer side of rectangle, roll dough tightly into a long roll. Press edges together to seal. Cut each roll into 12 slices. Place one slice in each muffin-pan with waxed paper and a towel and let dough rise until doubled.
18. Bake at 375°F 15 to 20 min. Invert muffin pans on cooling rack; let pan remain a minute so butter-sugar mixture drizzles down over rolls. Remove pan and cool rolls.

2 doz. Schnecken

Almond Snails: Substitute **toasted almonds** for pecan halves.

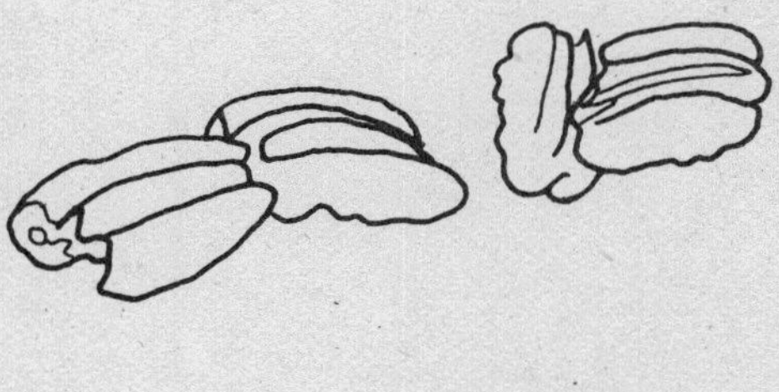

Stollen

1⅓ cups (about 7 oz.) almonds
1 cup (about 5 oz.) golden or dark raisins
½ cup (about 3 oz.) currants
1 cup (about 7 oz.) chopped citron
1 tablespoon grated lemon peel
1 cup milk
2 pkgs. active dry yeast
½ cup warm water, 110°F to 115°F (Or if using compressed yeast, soften 2 cakes in ½ cup lukewarm water, 80°F to 85°F.)
1 cup sugar
1 cup butter, softened
2 teaspoons salt
8 cup sifted all-purpose flour
1 teaspoon nutmeg
3 eggs, well beaten
Melted butter
1½ cups sifted confectioners' sugar
¾ teaspoon vanilla extract
3 tablespoons milk or cream (just enough to make frosting of spreading consistency)

Two 15½ x 12 in. baking sheets will be needed.

1. Blanch, toast and chop almonds.
2. Reserve ⅓ cup of the almonds for topping; mix remainder with golden or dark raisins, currants, chopped citron, and grated lemon peel. Set nut-fruit mixture aside.
3. Scald milk.
4. Meanwhile, soften yeast in water. Set aside.
5. Put sugar, butter, and salt into a large bowl.
6. Pour scalded milk over ingredients in bowl and stir mixture until butter is completely melted.
7. When lukewarm, blend in 1 cup of flour and nutmeg, beating until smooth. Stir softened yeast and add, mixing well.
8. Measure 6 to 7 cups of flour and add about one-half the flour to the dough and beat until very smooth. Add eggs in thirds, beating well after each addition.
9. Add the reserved nut-fruit mixture and mix thoroughly. Mix in enough of the remaining flour to make a soft dough. Turn dough onto a lightly floured surface and allow it to rest 5 to 10 min.
10. Knead dough. Form dough into a smooth ball and place it in a lightly greased, deep bowl. Turn dough to bring greased surface to top. Cover bowl with waxed paper and towel and let stand in warm place (about 80°F) until dough is doubled (about 2½ hrs).
11. Punch down dough with fist; pull edges in to center and turn dough completely over in bowl. Cover bowl with waxed paper and towel and let dough rise again until nearly doubled (about 1½ hrs).
12. Again punch down dough and turn out onto a lightly floured surface. Divide into two portions and shape each into a smooth ball.
13. Allow dough to rest 5 to 10 min.
14. Meanwhile, lightly grease the baking sheets.
15. Roll or pat out each ball of dough into an oval 13 in. long and about 1 in. thick. With rolling pin, flatten and press one lengthwise half of oval about ½ in. thick. Turn unflattened half of dough over flattened half; lightly press edges together. Press the fold down firmly with palm of hand; this helps to prevent dough from springing open during rising. Repeat to shape second oval.
16. Place one Stollen on each baking sheet. Brush tops with butter.
17. Cover with waxed paper and towel and let rise in warm place until doubled (about 1½ hrs).
18. Bake at 325°F about 30 min., or until Stollen are light golden brown.
19. While Stollen are baking, prepare the frosting by combining sugar and vanilla extract.
20. Add milk or cream gradually, blending after each addition.
21. Remove baked Stollen to cooling racks. Immediately spread frosting over tops. Sprinkle reserved almonds over frosting.

2 large Stollen

Note: The addition of a few finely cut **candied cherries** to the nut-fruit mixture adds a touch of color.

Filled Berlin Doughnuts (Bismarcks)

1 cup milk
1 pkg. active dry yeast
¼ cup warm water, 110°F to 115°F (Or if using compressed yeast, soften 1 cake in ¼ cup lukewarm water, 80°F to 85°F.)
½ cup sugar
⅓ cup butter
1 tablespoon orange juice
2 teaspoons rum extract
1 teaspoon salt
4 cup sifted all-purpose flour
2 eggs, well beaten
Sugar

A deep saucepan for deep-frying or an automatic deep-fryer will be needed.

1. Scald milk
2. Meanwhile, soften yeast in water. Set aside.
3. Put sugar, butter, orange juice, rum extract, and salt into a large bowl.
4. Immediately pour scalded milk over ingredients in bowl. When lukewarm, blend in 1 cup of flour beating until smooth. Stir softened yeast and add, mixing well.
5. Measure 2½ - 3 cups of flour.
6. Add about one-half the flour to the yeast mixture and beat until very smooth. Beat in 2 eggs. Then beat in enough remaining flour to make a soft dough. Turn dough onto a lightly floured surface and allow it to rest 5 to 10 min.
7. Knead. Form dough into a large ball and place in a greased, deep bowl. Turn dough to bring greased surface to top. Cover with waxed paper and towel and let stand in a warm place (about 80°F) until dough is doubled.
8. Punch down dough with fist. Turn dough out onto lightly floured surface and roll ½ in. thick. Cut dough into rounds with a 3-in. cookie cutter. Cover with waxed paper and let rise on rolling surface, away from drafts and direct heat, 15 to 30 min. or until doubled.
9. About 20 min. before deep-frying, fill the saucepan or fryer with fat and heat to 365°F.
10. Deep-fry doughnuts in heated fat. Fry only as many doughnuts at one time as will float uncrowded one layer deep in the fat. Fry 2 to 3 min., or until lightly browned. Turn doughnuts with a fork or tongs when they rise to the surface and several times during cooking; do not pierce. Lift from fat with tongs or slotted spoon. Drain doughnuts over fat for a few seconds before removing to absorbent paper. Cool completely.
11. Cut a slit through to the center in the side of each cooled doughnut. Force about ½ teaspoon of jam or jelly into center and press lightly to close slit. (A pastry bag and tube may be used to force jelly or jam into slit.) Shake 2 to 3 Bismarcks at one time in plastic bag containing sugar.

About 1½ doz. doughnuts

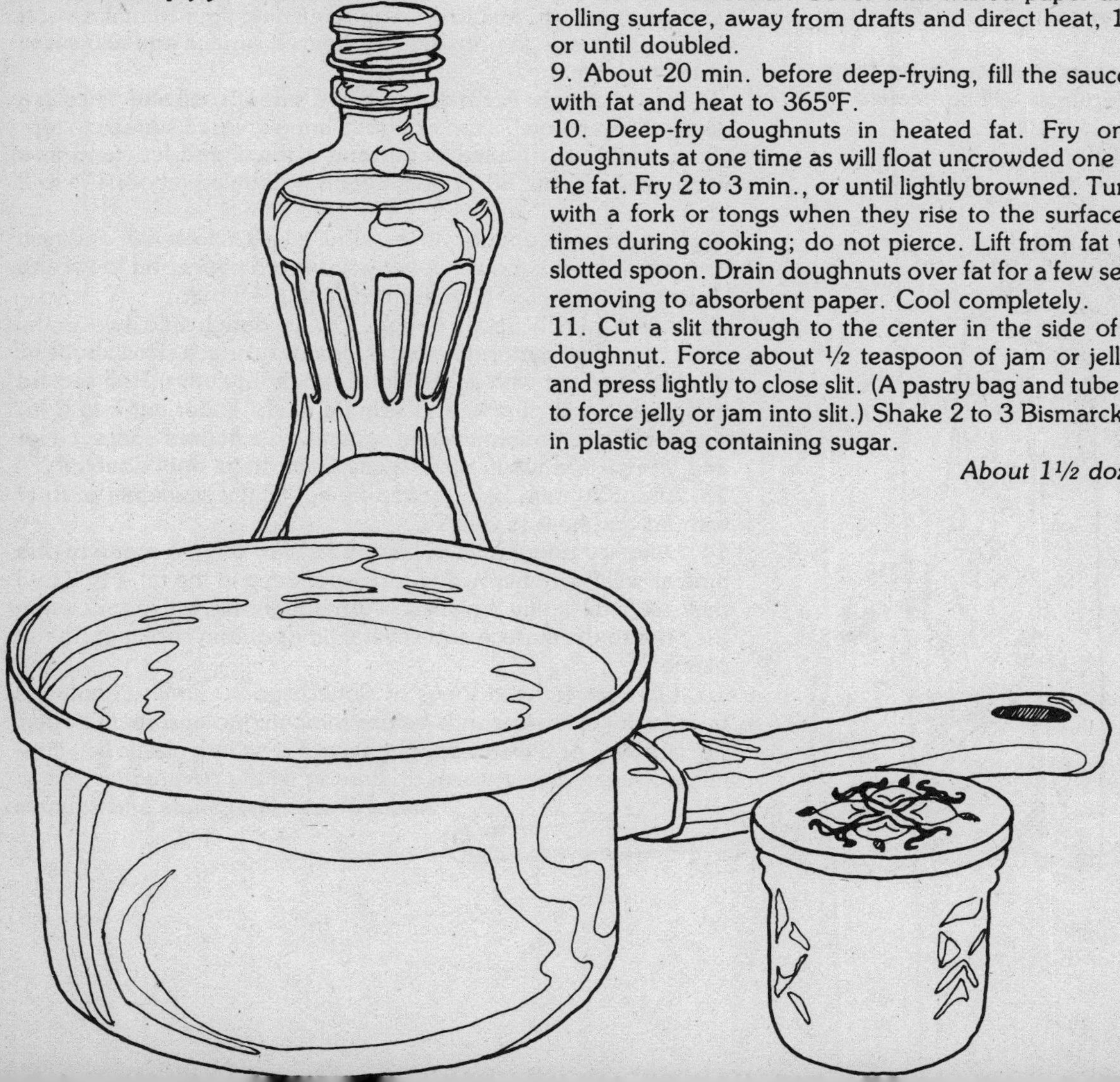

Potato Doughnuts

- **3 medium-size (about 1 lb.) potatoes**
- **2 pkgs. active dry yeast**
- **½ cup warm water, 110°F to 115°F (Or if using compressed yeast, soften 2 cakes in ½ cup lukewarm water, 80°F to 85°F).**
- **2 tablespoons sugar**
- **6 cups sifted all-purpose flour**
- **½ cup softened butter**
- **2 eggs, well beaten**
- **½ cup plus 2 tablespoons sugar**
- **1 tablespoon grated lemon peel**
- **1½ teaspoons salt**
- **¾ teaspoon nutmeg**
- **½ cup sugar**

A deep saucepan for deep-frying or an automatic deep-fryer will be needed.

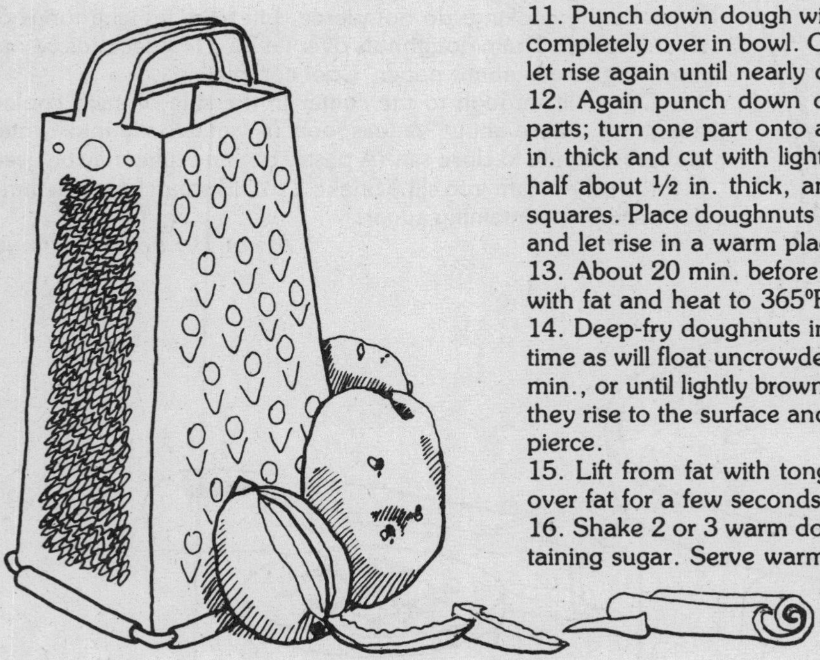

1. Wash, pare and cook potatoes.
2. Cook about 25 to 35 min., or until tender when pierced with a fork. Drain, reserving 1 cup cooking liquid. Dry potatoes by shaking pan over low heat. Cover potatoes and keep warm; set aside.
3. Soften yeast in water. Set aside.
4. When reserved cooking liquid has cooled to lukewarm, pour it into a large bowl. Stir in 2 tablespoons of sugar.
5. Stir softened yeast and add to mixture, mixing well. Add and beat 2 cups of flour until mixture is smooth.
6. Cover bowl with waxed paper and a towel and let stand in a warm place (about 80°F) until very light and bubbly (about 1 hr.).
7. Meanwhile, mash potatoes. Measure 1 cup mashed potatoes. Put into a bowl; beat in butter, eggs and a mixture of sugar, grated lemon peel, salt, and nutmeg.
8. When yeast mixture becomes very bubbly, stir in potato mixture. Measure 4 to 5 cups of flour.
9. Add about one-half of flour to yeast-potato mixture and beat until very smooth. Mix in enough remaining flour to make a soft dough. Turn dough onto a lightly floured surface and allow it to rest 5 to 10 min.
10. Knead dough. Form dough into a smooth ball and place in a greased, deep bowl. Turn dough to bring greased surface to top. Cover bowl with waxed paper and a towel and let stand in a warm place (about 80°F) until dough is doubled (about 1½ to 2 hrs.).
11. Punch down dough with fist. Pull edges in to center and turn completely over in bowl. Cover with waxed paper and towel and let rise again until nearly doubled (about 45 min.).
12. Again punch down dough. Divide dough into two equal parts; turn one part onto a lightly floured surface. Roll about ½ in. thick and cut with lightly flour doughnut cutter. Roll second half about ½ in. thick, and using a sharp knife, cut into 2-in. squares. Place doughnuts and squares on a floured board; cover and let rise in a warm place away from drafts until doubled.
13. About 20 min. before deep-frying, fill the saucepan or fryer with fat and heat to 365°F.
14. Deep-fry doughnuts in heated fat. Fry only as many at one time as will float uncrowded one layer deep in the fat. Fry 2 to 3 min., or until lightly browned. Turn doughnuts with a fork when they rise to the surface and several times during cooking; do not pierce.
15. Lift from fat with tongs or slotted spoon. Drain doughnuts over fat for a few seconds before removing to absorbent paper.
16. Shake 2 or 3 warm doughnuts at a time in a plastic bag containing sugar. Serve warm or store in tightly covered jar.

About 3 doz. doughnuts and squares

Quick Coffee Cake

For Topping:

1/3 cup sugar
1 1/2 teaspoons cinnamon
1/3 cup (about 1 oz.) chopped walnuts
1 tablespoons butter, melted

For Cake:

1 cup sifted all-purpose flour
1/2 cup sugar
1 1/2 teaspoons baking powder
1/2 teaspoon salt

1/4 cup butter

1 egg, well beaten
1/2 cup milk

Grease an 8-in. round layer cake pan.

1. For Topping—Mix together in order sugar, cinnamon chopped walnuts, and butter. Set aside.
2. For Cake—Sift together flour, sugar, baking powder, and salt.
3. Cut butter in with pastry blender or 2 knives until pieces are size of rice kernels.
4. Make a well in center of dry ingredients and add, all at one time, a mixture of egg and milk.
5. Stir, mixing only enough to moisten dry ingredients, about 15 strokes. Turn batter into pan and spread evenly to edges. Sprinkle topping over surface and gently pat down with back of a spoon or fork.
6. Bake at 375°F about 20 min., or until a wooden pick or cake tester comes out clean when inserted gently in center of coffee cake. Serve coffe cake hot.

6 servings

Orange Coffee Cake: Substitute grated **orange peel** for cinnamon in topping. For cake decrease milk to 1/3 cup and add 3 tablespoons **orange juice.**

Main Dishes

Pork, veal, poultry and fish are widely used in Middle Europe. Because Central Europeans regard the sheep as a wool-producing animal and the cow as a milk rather than a meat-producing animal, lamb is rarely available and the beef which finds its way to market is of the less-tender variety. Nevertheless the German homemaker has created from the beef at her disposal one of the finest dishes in the world—sauerbraten. Goose and duckling are as popular as chicken is in this country, and throughout Germany and Austria roast goose is a traditional Christmas holiday bird. Sweet-sour red cabbage or sauerkraut and dumplings (of course) are the traditional accompaniments for the meat course.

Pot Roast of Beef with Wine

- **3 lb. boneless pot roast of beef (rump, chuck or round)**
- **4 cups red wine**
- **2 medium-size onions, chopped**
- **3 medium-size carrots, washed, pared and sliced**
- **1 clove garlic**
- **1 bay leaf**
- **¼ teaspoon pepper**
- **4 sprigs parsley**
- **½ cup all-purpose flour**
- **2 teaspoons salt**
- **¼ teaspoon pepper**
- **3 tablespoons butter**
- **1 cup cold water**

1. Put the meat into a deep bowl. Add 2 cups of red wine, onions, carrots, garlic, bay leaf, ¼ teaspoon pepper and parsley.
2. Cover and put into refrigerator to marinate 12 hrs., or overnight. Turn meat occasionally. Drain the meat, reserving marinade, and pat meat dry with absorbent paper.
3. Coat meat evenly with a mixture of flour, salt and ¼ teaspoon pepper.
4. Heat butter in a Dutch oven or large, heavy sauce pot. Brown the meat slowly on all sides in the butter. Drain off the fat. Add the marinade and 2 cups of wine.
5. Cover and bring to boiling. Reduce heat and simmer slowly 2½ to 3 hrs., or until meat is tender. Remove meat to a warm platter.
6. Strain the liquid. Return the strained liquid to the Dutch oven or sauce pot.
7. Pour water into a screw-top jar and sprinkle flour onto water. Cover jar tightly and shake until mixture is well blended.
8. Stirring; constantly, slowly pour one half of the blended mixture into liquid in Dutch oven. Bring to boiling. Gradually add only what is needed of the remaining blended mixture for consistency desired. Bring gravy to boiling after each addition. Cook 3 to 5 min. longer. Serve meat with gravy, buttered carrots and potato dumplings.

8 to 10 servings

Marinated Beef

- **4 lb. blade pot roast of beef (any beef pot roast may be used)**
- **2 cups vinegar**
- **2 cups water**
- **1 large onion, sliced**
- **¼ cup sugar**
- **2 teaspoons salt**
- **10 peppercorns**
- **3 whole cloves**
- **2 bay leaves**
- **1 lemon, rinsed and cut into ¼-in. slices**
- **2 tablespoons butter**
- **¼ cup butter**
- **¼ cup all-purpose flour**
- **3 cups liquid (reserved cooking liquid and enough reserved marinade or hot water to equal 3 cups liquid)**
- **½ cup thick sour cream**

A heavy 4-qt. kettle or Dutch oven having a tight-fitting cover will be needed. Set out a deep 3- or 4-qt. bowl.

1. Have ready 4-lb. blade pot roast of beef. Put the meat into the bowl. Set aside.
2. Combine in a saucepan and heat without boiling vinegar, water, onion, sugar, salt, peppercorns, cloves, and bay leaves.
3. Pour hot mixture over meat in bowl and allow to cool. Add lemon.
4. Cover and set in refrigerator. Marinate for 4 days, turning meat once each day.
5. Set out the kettle and a tight-fitting cover.
6. Remove meat from marinade and drain thoroughly. Strain and reserve marinade.
7. Heat butter in the kettle over low heat.
8. Add the pot roast and brown slowly on all sides over medium heat. Slowly add 2 cups of the reserved marinade (reserve remaining marinade for gravy). Bring liquid to boiling. Reduce heat; cover kettle tightly and simmer 2½ to 3 hrs., or until meat is tender when pierced with a fork. Add more of the marinade if necessary. Liquid surrounding meat should at all times be simmering, not boiling.
9. Remove meat to a warm platter and keep warm. Pour cooking liquid from kettle and set aside for gravy. For gravy melt butter in the kettle. Blend in ¼ cup of flour.
10. Heat until butter-flour mixture bubbles and is golden brown, stirring constantly. Remove kettle from heat.
11. Add liquid gradually, stirring constantly.
12. Return to heat. Bring to boiling; cook rapidly, stirring constantly, until gravy thickens. Cook 1 to 2 min. longer. Remove from heat. Stirring vigorously with a French whip, whisk beater, or fork, add sour cream to kettle in very small amounts.
13. Cook mixture over low heat about 3 to 5 min., stirring constantly, until thoroughly heated; do not boil. Serve meat and gravy with potato pancakes.

8 to 10 servings

Marinated Beef with Noodles: Omit gravy and Potato Pancakes. Serve with **Buttered Noodles.**

Marinated Beef with Raisins: Stir into gravy with the sour cream ½ cup (about 3 oz.) dark **seedless raisins.**

Marinated Beef with Garlic: Before marinating the beef, rub the surface all over with the cut surfaces of 1 clove **garlic.**

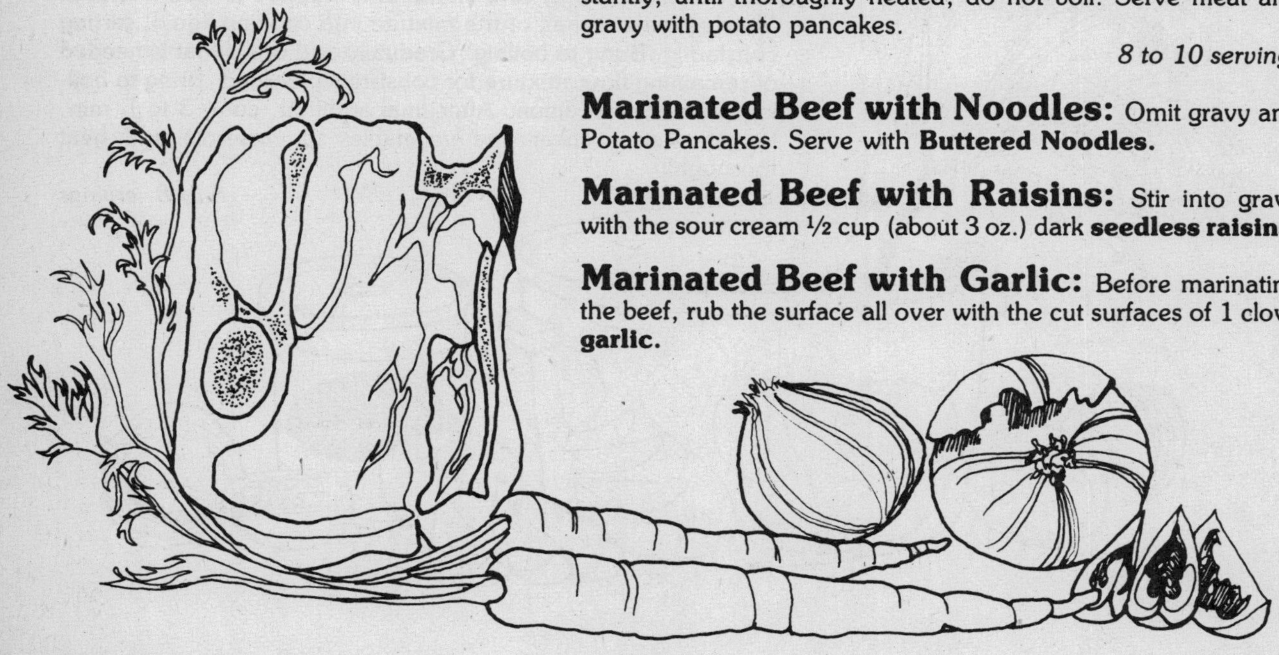

Oxtail Stew

- **3 oxtails (about 1 lb. each), disjointed**
- **½ cup all-purpose flour**
- **1 teaspoon salt**
- **¼ teaspoon pepper**
- **1½ cups (about 3 medium-size) chopped onion**
- **3 tablespoons butter**
- **1 28 oz. can tomatoes**
- **1½ cups hot water**
- **4 medium-size (about 1½ lbs.) potatoes**
- **6 medium-size carrots**
- **2 lbs. fresh peas**
- **1 tablespoon paprika**
- **1 teaspoon salt**
- **¼ teaspoon pepper**
- **¼ cup water**
- **2 tablespoons all-purpose flour**

1. Set out a 3-qt. top-of-range casserole having a tight-fitting cover.
2. Have oxtails ready. Coat pieces evenly by shaking 2 or 3 at a time in a plastic bag containing a mixture of flour, salt, and pepper.
3. Prepare onion.
4. Heat butter in the casserole over low heat.
5. Add the onion and cook over medium heat until almost tender, occasionally moving and turning with a spoon. Remove onion with a slotted spoon and set aside. Put meat into casserole and brown on all sides.
6. Meanwhile, drain tomatoes, reserving liquid. Cut tomatoes into pieces; set aside.
7. Return onion to casserole. Add the reserved tomato liquid and 1½ cups of water.
8. Cover tightly and simmer 2½ to 3 hrs., until meat is nearly tender when pierced with a fork.
9. When meat has cooked 2 hrs., wash and pare potatoes.
10. Rinse and pare or scrape carrots.
11. Using a ball-shaped cutter, cut the potatoes and carrots into small balls.
12. Rinse and shell peas.
13. When meat is almost tender, add the potato and carrot balls, peas, and a mixture of paprika, salt, and pepper.
14. Cover and simmer 20 min. longer, or until vegetables are nearly tender. Add the tomatoes and cook 10 min. longer or until meat and vegetables are tender. Remove meat and vegetables to a warm dish.
15. Pour ¼ cup of water into a screw-top jar.
16. Sprinkle flour onto the liquid.
17. Cover jar tightly and shake until mixture is well blended. Slowly pour one-half of the mixture into cooking liquid, stirring constantly. Bring to boiling. Gradually add only what is needed of remaining flour mixture for consistency desired. Bring to boiling after each addition. After final addition, cook 3 to 5 min. longer. Return meat and vegetables to casserole and heat thoroughly.

6 to 8 servings

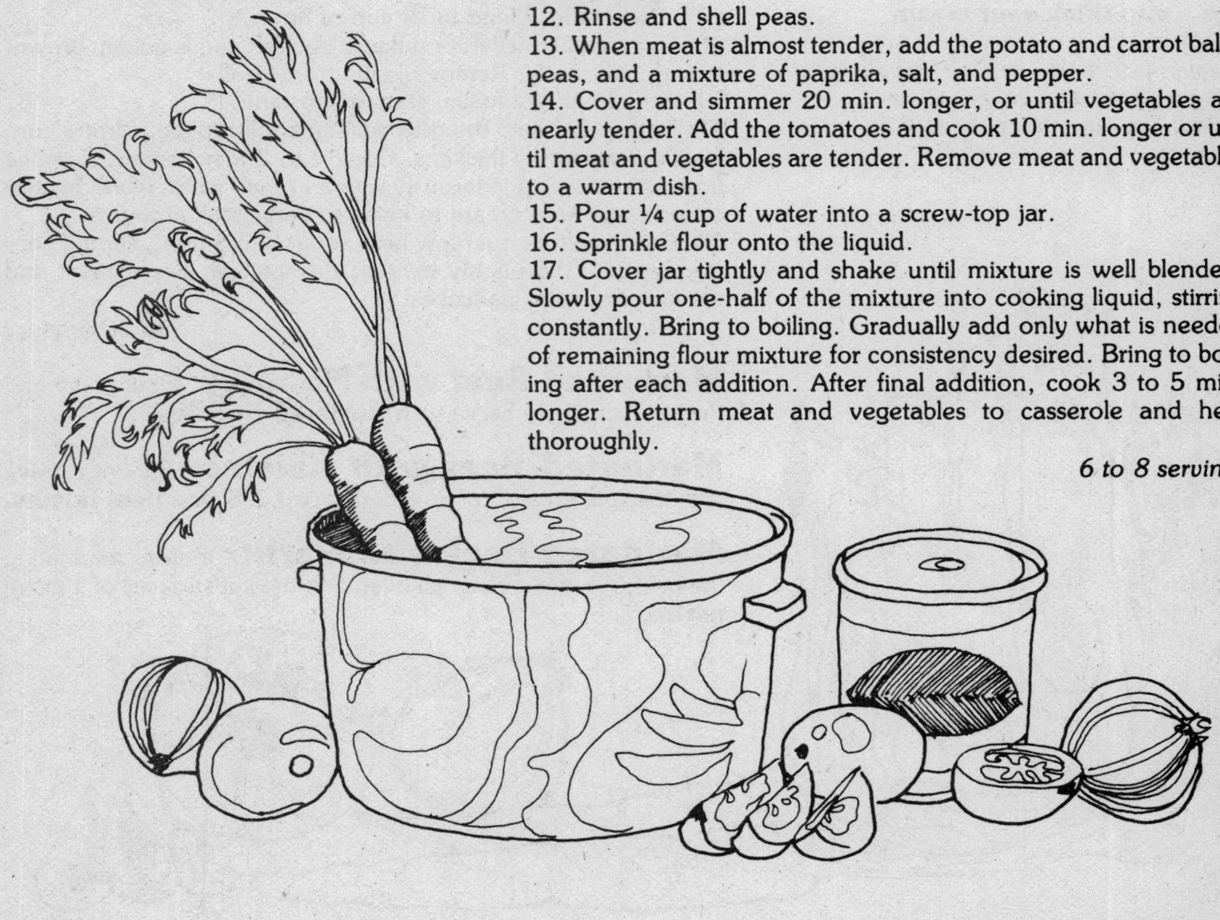

Koenigsberg Meat Balls

- **1 cup soft bread crumbs**
- **¼ cup milk**
- **1 medium-size onion**
- **2 tablespoons butter**
- **1 lb. beef, ground twice**
- **¼ lb. veal, ground twice**
- **4 anchovy fillets, mashed**
- **1 egg, beaten**
- **1 teaspoon salt**
- **¼ teaspoon pepper**
- **3 cups water**
- **2 tablespoons chopped onion**
- **1 bay leaf**
- **1 whole clove**
- **2 peppercorns**
- **¼ teaspoon salt**
- **2 tablespoons butter**
- **2 tablespoons all-purpose flour**
- **2 tablespoons lemon juice**
- **1 tablespoon capers, chopped**

1. Set out a 2-qt. saucepan.
2. Put bread crumbs and milk into a large bowl.
3. Clean and chop onion.
4. Heat butter in a skillet.
5. Add the onion and cook over medium heat until the onion is golden, moving and turning with a spoon. Add the contents of the skillet to the bowl with beef, veal, anchovy fillets, and egg, and a mixture of salt and pepper.
6. Combine lightly but thoroughly. Shape into balls about 2 in. in diameter.
7. Bring water, onion, bay leaf, clove, peppercorns, and salt to boiling in the saucepan.
8. Carefully put the meat balls into the liquid. Bring to boiling; reduce heat and simmer 20 min. Remove the balls with a slotted spoon and set aside to keep warm.
9. Strain liquid. Heat butter in the saucepan.
10. Blend in flour.
11. Heat until mixture bubbles. Remove from heat. Gradually add 2 cups of liquid and lemon juice and capers.
12. Bring rapidly to boiling, stirring constantly. Cook 1 to 2 min. longer. Return the meat balls to the sauce and heat thoroughly.
13. Serve with **Buttered Noodles** allowing 2 or 3 balls to each serving.

6 to 8 servings

Pheasant

- **1 Pheasant**
- **1- 1½ teaspoons salt**
- **½ teaspoon black pepper**
- **8 medium peeled raw potatoes**
- **1- 1½ teaspoons salt**
- **3 tablespoons butter**
- **¾ cup heavy cream**
- **1 oz. apple cheese**
- **2 teaspoons soy sauce**
- **1 large bunch parsley sprigs**

1. Rinse and wipe the pheasant inside and outside. Season with salt and pepper, half inside and half outside. Brown the pheasant quickly all around in a frying pan in half the butter. Wrap in aluminum foil.
2. Preheat the oven to 325°F.
3. Cut the peeled raw potatoes in slices and fry them lightly on both sides in the remaining butter in the pan. Later add the rest of the butter. Sprinkle some salt over each round of potato slices before they are transferred to an ovenproof deep dish or casserole.
4. Distribute the potato slices evenly on the bottom and up towards the edge of the casserole, place the pheasant in the middle and pour on the gravy from foil if there is any.
5. Cover the casserole immediately. Put the casserole in the oven and roast the pheasant for about 30 minutes.
6. Whip together cream, apple cheese and soy sauce. Taste and correct seasoning, adding more apple cheese if necessary.
7. Pour the cream mixture on pheasant and potatoes when the casserole has been in the oven for 20 minutes. Serve dish straight from the oven with the pheasant cut in four portion sizes, and garnish with fresh parsley sprigs.

4 servings

Puffy Veal Cutlets

- **1½ lbs. veal round steak (cutlet), cut about ½ in. thick**
- **¼ cup all-purpose flour**
- **1 teaspoon salt**
- **1/8 teaspoon pepper**
- **1 egg yolk**
- **4 tablespoons butter**
- **1 egg white**

1. Set out a large, heavy skillet having a tight-fitting cover.
2. Have steak ready.
3. Cut into 4 serving-size pieces. Coat cutlets with a mixture of flour, salt, and pepper. Set aside.
4. Beat egg yolk until thick and lemon-colored.
5. Set aside.
6. Heat butter in the skillet over low heat.
7. Meanwhile, using a clean beater, beat egg white until rounded peaks are formed.
8. Spread the egg yolk over the egg white and gently fold together.
9. Coat cutlets on one side with the egg mixture. Put cutlets into skillet egg-coated side down. Cook until lightly browned (about 15 min.).
10. Spoon remaining egg mixture onto cutlets, being sure to cover tops and turn. Cover and cook over low heat about 20 min., or until meat is tender when pierced with a fork.

4 servings

Veal Cutlets with Fried Eggs: Do not separate egg; beat slightly and mix with 1 tablespoon **milk.** After flouring cutlets, dip into the egg mixture and then coat with 1 cup (3 to 4 slices) fine, dry **bread crumbs.** Cook; keep warm while preparing fried eggs.

1. Heat 1 to 2 tablespoons **butter** in a heavy skillet over low heat. Break into a saucer, one at a time, and slip into the skillet, 4 **eggs.** Reduce heat and cook slowly about 4 min., or to desired stage of firmness. Baste eggs frequently with butter in skillet.
2. Arrange fried eggs on top of cutlets. Garnish platter with vegetables and diamonds of crisp toast topped with smoked salmon, caviar and cutouts of hard-cooked egg white.

American-Style Wiener Schnitzel: Follow recipe for Veal Cutlets with Fried Eggs; omit fried eggs. Melt over low heat 2 tablespoons **butter.** Stir in 6 **anchovy fillets,** mashed, and 1 tablespoon **lemon juice.** Pour over the cutlets. Garnish with **parsley.**

Schnitzel with Spinach

2½ lbs. veal cutlet
½ teaspoon salt
½ teaspoon pepper
2 lb. spinach
2 tablespoons butter
¼ teaspoon nutmeg
¾ cup beef bouillon
2 sprigs tarragon, chopped

Piquant Sauce:

1 large onion, chopped
3 tablespoons green pepper, finely chopped
1 tablespoons fresh tarragon or 1 teaspoon dried tarragon
4 tablespoons tomato paste
½-¾ cup white wine
½-¾ cup concentrated beef bouillon
½-¾ cup heavy cream
⅛ teaspoon arrow root

1. Make sauce. Saute onion, green pepper, tarragon and tomato paste in butter. Add wine and bouillon. Cook covered over low heat for 30 minutes. Strain sauce and return to saucepan. Add cream and arrow root and season with salt and pepper. Keep sauce warm.
2. Heat butter and saute veal over low heat about 5 minutes. Add bouillon and continue to cook about 10 minutes. Turn a few times.
3. Chop and saute spinach in butter. Season with salt and nutmeg.
4. Place spinach on serving dish and put veal on top. Pour sauce on top. Garnish with tarragon. Serve with cooked rice.

8 servings

Pork Chops with Ham and Cheese

2 pork chops
¼ teaspoon salt
⅛ teaspoon pepper or ⅛ teaspoon paprika
½ teaspoon tarragon, oregano or rosemary
3 slices bayonne ham
2 slices cheese, cheddar
1 lb. can ratatouille
1-2 tablespoons dry red or white wine

1. Brown pork chops about 20 minutes and season. Place ham and grated cheese on top.
2. Heat vegetables and add wine. Place in ovenproof dish with pork chops on top. Bake in 475°F. for 5-10 minutes.

2 servings

Roast Loin of Pork

3½ -lb. (8 ribs) pork loin roast
1½ teaspoons onion salt
½ teaspoon marjoram, crushed
¼ teaspoon pepper

1. Rub roast with a mixture of the salt, marjoram, and pepper. Secure roast on spit. Insert meat thermometer. Adjust spit about 8 inches above prepared coals, placing aluminum foil pan under pork to catch drippings. If using a gas-fired grill, adjust flame size following manufacturer's directions.
2. Roast until meat thermometer registers 170°F. or until meat is tender. About 30 minutes before roast is done, score surface.
3. Place roast on a warm serving platter. Garnish with parsley.

Note: To roast in the oven, place pork loin, fat side up, on a rack in a shallow roasting pan. Roast, uncovered, at 325°F about 2½ hours.

Braised Spicy Spareribs

2 sections (about 4 lbs.) spareribs, cracked through center
1/3 cup all-purpose flour
2 teaspoons salt
1/4 teaspoon pepper
3 tablespoons fat
1 1/2 cups Quick Meat Broth
1/4 cup ketchup
3 tablespoons Worcestershire sauce
2 tablespoons vinegar
1/2 teaspoon celery salt
1/8 teaspoon cayenne pepper
3 whole cloves
3 whole allspice
1/2 bay leaf
1/2 clove garlic, minced
1 medium-size onion
1/4 cup cold water
2 tablespoons all-purpose flour

1. Set out a heavy skillet and a roasting pan having a tight-fitting cover.
2. *For Ribs*—Have spareribs ready.
3. Cut into serving-size pieces. Coat meat evenly with a mixture of flour, salt, and pepper.
4. Melt fat in the heavy skillet.
5. Add ribs to fat and brown slowly on both sides.
6. While meat is browning, prepare broth.
7. Mix into meat broth ketchup, Worcestershire sauce, vinegar, celery salt, cayenne pepper, cloves, allspice, bay leaf, and garlic.
8. Clean and finely chop onion.
9. Put meat into the roasting pan. Pour broth mixture over browned ribs. Add chopped onion. Cover and put in 350°F oven for about 1½ hrs., or until ribs are tender.
10. With a slotted spoon, remove meat from pan to a warm serving platter. Set aside to keep warm while preparing sauce.
11. *For Sauce*—If necessary, skim excess fat from cooking liquid. Strain the liquid and pour into a small saucepan.
12. Put water into a 1-pt. screw-top jar.
13. Sprinkle 2 tablespoons all-purpose flour onto it.
14. Cover jar tightly and shake until mixture is well blended.
15. Bring liquid in saucepan to boiling; stirring constantly, slowly pour one-half of the flour mixture into cooking liquid. Bring to boiling. Gradually add only what is needed of the remaining flour mixture for consistency desired. Bring sauce to boiling after each addition. Cook 3 to 5 min.
16. Spoon or pour about one-half of the hot sauce over spareribs on the platter. Serve remaining sauce in a gravy boat if desired.

4 to 6 servings

Spareribs and Sauerkraut

3 lbs. spareribs, cracked through center
Water to barely cover
1/2 teaspoon salt
1 27 oz. can (about 3½ cups) sauerkraut

1. Set out a large sauce pot or kettle having a tight-fitting cover.
2. Have spareribs ready.
3. Cut into serving-size pieces. Put spareribs into the sauce pot with water.
4. Add contents of sauerkraut.
5. Cover and bring liquid rapidly to boiling. Reduce heat and simmer 1½ to 2 hrs., or until meat is tender. Drain slightly and remove to a heated platter. Serve spareribs with the sauerkraut and with potatoes and beets.

About 6 servings

Spareribs and Sauerkraut with Caraway Seeds: Add and mix in with the sauerkraut before cooking 1 teaspoon **caraway seeds.**

Sweet-Sour Sausage Links

- **16 sausage links (about 1 lb.)**
- **2 tablespoons cold water**
- **1 medium-size onion**
- **2 tablespoons reserved sausage drippings**
- **2 tablespoons all-purpose flour**
- **1 cup hot water**
- **2 tablespoons vinegar**
- **2 tablespoons brown sugar**
- **1/4 teaspoon salt**
- **1/8 teaspoon pepper**

1. Put sausage links into a large, cold skillet.
2. Add water.
3. If skillet will not hold entire amount of sausage, cook one half at a time. Cover and cook slowly 8 to 10 min. Remove cover and pour off liquid. Brown links over medium heat, turning as necessary (do not prick links with fork). Pour off fat as it collects; reserve fat.
4. Meanwhile, clean and chop onion.
5. When sausage links are browned, remove from skillet. Drain on absorbent paper. Set aside to keep warm.
6. Put onion in hot skillet containing drippings.
7. Cook over medium heat until onion is soft. Blend in flour.
8. Heat until mixture bubbles. Remove from heat and add water, vinegar, brown sugar, salt and pepper gradually, stirring constantly.
9. Bring to boiling. Reduce heat and cook 1 to 2 min. Return sausages to the sauce and cook over low heat 10 min., or until thoroughly heated.

4 servings

Marinated Rabbit Stew

- **1 rabbit, 2½ to 3 lbs., ready-to-cook weight**
- **3 cups red wine vinegar**
- **3 cups water**
- **½ cup sugar**
- **1 medium-size onion, sliced**
- **2 carrots, washed, pared and cut into pieces**
- **1 tablespoon salt**
- **1 teaspoon pickling spices**
- **1/4 teaspoon pepper**
- **1/3 cup all-purpose flour**
- **1 teaspoon salt**
- **1/4 teaspoon pepper**
- **3 tablespoons fat**
- **1/4 cup all-purpose flour**

1. A Dutch oven or a large, heavy sauce pot having a tight-fitting cover will be needed.
2. Clean and cut rabbit into serving-size pieces.
3. (If frozen, thaw according to directions on the package.) Put rabbit pieces into a deep bowl and cover with a mixture of vinegar, water, sugar, onion, carrots, 1 tablespoon salt, pickling spices and 1/4 teaspoon pepper.
4. Cover and put into refrigerator 2 to 3 days to marinate. Turn rabbit pieces often.
5. Drain rabbit pieces, reserving marinade. Dry on absorbent paper. Strain the marinade. Coat rabbit pieces evenly by shaking two or three at a time in a plastic bag containing a mixture of 1/3l cup all-purpose flour, 1 teaspoon salt, and 1/4 teaspoon pepper.
6. Heat fat in the Dutch oven or sauce pot.
7. Add the rabbit pieces and brown slowly, turning to brown evenly. Remove from heat. Gradually add 2 cups of the marinade. Cover and simmer 45 min. to 1 hr., or until meat is tender.
8. Pour into a screw-top jar ½ cup of the reserved marinade. Sprinkle 1/4 cup all-purpose flour onto the liquid.
9. Cover jar tightly and shake until mixture is well blended. Slowly pour one half of the mixture into cooking liquid, stirring constantly. Bring to boiling. Gradually add only what is needed of remaining mixture for consistency desired. Bring to boiling after each addition. After final addition, cook 3 to 5 min.
10. Arrange the rabbit pieces on a serving platter. Pour some of the gravy over the rabbit and serve with the remaining gravy.

6 servings

Macaroni and Ham

- **3 qts. water**
- **1 tablespoon salt**
- **2 cups (8-oz. pkg.) uncooked macaroni (elbows or other shapes, or tubes broken into 2-in. pieces)**
- **2 cups Thin White Sauce (double recipe, page 39; mix 1/4 teaspoon dry mustard and a dash of paprika with flour before blending into fat; add 1/2 teaspoon Worcestershire sauce with the milk)**
- **4 oz. sharp Cheddar cheese (1 cup, grated)**
- **1/4 cup minced onion**
- **1 cup diced cooked ham**

1. Lightly butter a 1 1/2-qt. casserole.
2. Heat water and salt to boiling in a large saucepan.
3. Add macaroni gradually.
4. Boil rapidly, uncovered, 10 to 15 min. Test tenderness by pressing a piece against side of pan with fork or spoon. Drain macaroni by turning it into a colander or large sieve; rinse with hot water to remove loose starch.
5. Meanwhile, prepare and set aside Thin White Sauce.
6. Grate and set aside cheese.
7. Prepare onion and set aside.
8. Dice cooked ham.
9. Lightly but thoroughly mix together the ham, macaroni, sauce, 3/4 cup of the cheese and the minced onion. Turn into the buttered casserole. Sprinkle with the remaining cheese.
10. Bake at 350°F 25 to 30 min., or until top is lightly browned.

6 to 8 servings

Roast Goose with Prune-Apple Stuffing

- **2 cups pitted cooked prunes**
- **1 goose, 10 to 12 lbs., ready-to-cook weight**
- **Salt**
- **6 medium-size (about 2 lbs.) apples**

1. Set out a shallow roasting pan with rack.
2. Have prunes ready and reserve about 8 to 10 prunes for garnish.
3. Clean and remove any layers of fat from body cavity and opening of goose.
4. Cut off neck at body, leaving on neck skin. (If goose is frozen, thaw according to directions on package.) Rinse and pat dry with absorbent paper. (Reserve giblets for use in gravy or other food preparation.) Rub body and neck cavities of goose with salt.
5. Wash, quarter, core and pare apples.
6. Lightly fill body and neck cavities with the apples and prunes. To close body cavity, sew or skewer and lace with cord. Fasten neck skin to back with skewer. Loop cord around legs and tighten slightly. Place breast side down on rack in roasting pan.
7. Roast uncovered at 325°F 3 hrs. Remove fat from pan as it accumulates during this period. Turn goose breast side up. Roast 1 to 2 hrs. longer, or until goose tests done. To test for doneness, move leg gently by grasping end of bone; drumstick-thigh joint should move easily. (Protect fingers with paper napkin.) Allow about 25 min. per pound to estimate total roasting time.
8. To serve, remove skewers and cord. Place goose on heated platter. Remove some of the apples from goose and arrange on the platter. Garnish with the reserved prunes and **water cress.** For an attractive garnish, place cooked prunes on top of cooked apple rings, if desired.

8 servings

Roast Goose with Potato Stuffing: Omit apples and prunes. Prepare and lightly fill body and neck cavities with **Potato Stuffing.**

Potato Stuffing

3⅓ lbs. (about 10 medium-size) potatoes
1 cup (about 2 medium-size) chopped onion
⅔ cup chopped celery
½ cup fat
4 cups (about 6 slices) soft bread crumbs
2 eggs, beaten
1 tablespoon poultry seasoning
2 teaspoons salt
¼ teaspoon pepper

1. Wash, pare and cook potatoes.
2. Cook about 30 min., or until potatoes are tender when pierced with a fork. Drain. Dry potatoes by shaking pan over low heat.
3. Meanwhile, prepare onion and celery.
4. Heat fat in a skillet.
5. Add the onion and celery and cook over medium heat until vegetables are tender, occasionally moving and turning them with spoon. Remove skillet from heat; set aside.
6. Force potatoes through a food mill or ricer into a large bowl. Add cooked vegetables and bread crumbs.
7. Mix thoroughly; toss with a mixture of eggs, poultry seasoning, salt, and pepper.
8. Spoon stuffing into neck and body cavities of goose; do not pack. Stuff the goose just before roasting. Extra stuffing may be placed in greased baking dish and baked with goose the last hour of baking.

Enough stuffing for a 10- to 12-lb. goose

Loin of Venison

2 lb. boned loin of venison
3 tablespoons oil
¼ cup red wine
½ teaspoon black pepper
¼ cup cashews
⅓ cup raisins
2 tablespoons butter

Sauce

½ cup mushrooms, chopped
1½ teaspoons tomato paste
2 tablespoons oil
1 small yellow onion, diced
1 stalk celery, diced
1 red pepper, chopped
1 tablespoon flour
2½ cups beef stock
2 tablespoons parsley
1 bay leaf
½ cup red wine
2 tablespoons red wine vinegar
salt
½ teaspoon pepper
½ cup heavy cream

1. Cut venison into slices about ¼″ thick. Lay on a plate and sprinkle with 1 tbsp. oil and pepper. Cover and let stand for at least 1 hour.
2. Make sauce: Heat the oil, add onion, carrot, red pepper and celery and cook over a low heat until they start to brown.
3. Stir in the flour and continue cooking to a rich brown. Add ⅔ of the stock, the mushrooms, tomato paste, parsley and bay leaf and the wine. Bring mixture to a boil, stirring. Reduce heat and simmer with the lid half covering the pan for 20-25 minutes.
4. Add the remaining stock, bring to a boil again and skim. Strain sauce. Return to pan, add vinegar and continue to simmer 6-7 minutes.
5. Add cream and simmer for 5 minutes. Add nuts and raisins.
6. Heat remaining oil in a heavy frying pan and saute venison over a high heat for about 4 minutes on each side. Arrange on a warm platter and pour warm sauce on top.

4 servings

Stewed Chicken with Noodles

- **1 stewing chicken, 4 to 5 lbs., ready-to-cook weight**
- **Hot water to barely cover**
- **1 small onion**
- **3 sprigs parsley**
- **2 3-in. pieces celery with leaves**
- **1 bay leaf**
- **3 peppercorns**
- **2 teaspoons salt**
- **Buttered Noodles (page 37; use broad noodles)**
- **3 tablespoons butter or chicken fat**
- **3 tablespoons all-purpose flour**
- **3 cups cooled chicken broth**
- **2 teaspoons lemon juice**

1. Set out a kettle having a tight-fitting cover.
2. Rinse chicken. (If frozen, thaw according to directions on package.) Disjoint and cut into serving-size pieces. Rinse chicken pieces and giblets. Refrigerate the liver. Put chicken, gizzard, heart and neck into the kettle. (If desired, brown chicken pieces in a skillet with hot fat. Pieces may be coated with seasoned flour.) Add water.
3. Add onion, parsley, celery, bay leaf, peppercorns and salt to the water.
4. Bring water to boiling; remove foam. Cover kettle tightly, reduce heat, and simmer chicken 1 hr., skimming foam from surface as necessary. Continue cooking chicken 1 to 2 hrs. longer, or until thickest pieces are tender when pierced with a fork. During last 15 min. of cooking time, add liver to kettle. About 30 min. before chicken is tender, prepare noodles.
5. Arrange noodles on a warm serving platter. Remove chicken from broth and arrange on the noodles; keep warm. Strain broth and cool slightly; skim fat from surface.
6. *For Gravy*—Heat butter of chicken fat in a saucepan over low heat.
7. Blend in flour.
8. Heat until mixture bubbles. Remove from heat. Add gradually, stirring in broth and lemon juice. (Remaining chicken broth may be used in other food preparation.) Cook rapidly, stirring constantly, until mixture thickens. Cook 1 to 2 min. longer.
9. Pour over the chicken. Garnish with **parsley.**

About 6 servings

Chicken Fricassee: Add 1/4 teaspoon **thyme** with seasonings. Omit noodles. Clean and slice 1/4 lb. fresh **mushrooms.** Cook mushrooms in 2 tablespoons **butter,** moving and turning them with a spoon, until mushrooms are lightly browned. For gravy, use only 2 cups of the cooled chicken broth and 1 cup **cream.** Blend the lemon juice into thickened gravy and add cooked mushroom slices.

Chicken with Dumplings: Omit noodles. Prepare **Plain Dumplings** or **Herb Dumplings** (page 51) about 30 min. before chicken is tender. Add liver to kettle and mix in 1½ cups (16-oz. can, drained) **peas.** Drop dumpling batter by spoonfuls on top of chicken pieces. Dumplings should rest on top of chicken; if dumplings settle down into liquid, they may become soggy. If necessary, pour off excess liquid to prevent this. Cover tightly and continue cooking over medium heat 20 min. without removing cover. Remove dumplings and chicken to a warm serving dish; keep warm. Continue as in recipe; reserve peas when broth is strained. Return only 1½ cups peas to thickened gravy, reserving about ½ cup for garnish.

Baked Herring Casserole

2 salt herring
2 qts. cold water
6 medium-size (about 2 lbs.) potatoes
2 medium-size onions
2 egg yolks
1 cup thick sour cream
1 teaspoon salt
1/8 teaspoon pepper
1/3 cup buttered bread crumbs (page 8)

1. A 2-qt. casserole will be needed.
2. *To Prepare Herring*—With a sharp knife cut off and discard heads of herring.
3. Slit along underside of the fish from head to tail. Remove entrails and scrape insides well. Cut off tails and fins. Rinse thoroughly in cold water. Cut off and discard a 1/2-in. strip along each underside edge of fish. Make a slit along backbone just to the bone. Using a sharp knife, carefully pull and scrape the blue skin from the flesh. Be careful not to tear fish. Then cut along backbone through bone and flesh to remove one side of fish. Repeat for the second side. Remove as many of the small bones as possible without tearing fish.
4. Pour water into a large bowl.
5. Put herring into the water and set aside to soak 3 hrs.
6. *For Casserole*—Butter the casserole.
7. Wash, pare and cut potatoes into 1/4-in. slices.
8. Cook about 10 min,. or until potatoes are nearly tender. Drain potatoes and set aside.
9. Clean onions and chop.
10. Drain the herring, cut into small pieces and mix with the onion. Arrange a layer of potatoes in the casserole. Top with a layer of the fish-onion mixture. Repeat layers of potatoes and fish-onion mixture, ending with potatoes.
11. Beat egg yolks until thick and lemon-colored.
12. Stir in until blended a mixture of sour cream, salt and pepper.
13. Pour over the potatoes. Top with bread crumbs.
14. Bake at 350°F 35 to 40 min., or until lightly browned.

6 servings

Fresh Haddock, Hamburg Style: Omit salt herring. Cut into small pieces 2 lbs. dressed **haddock.** Combine with the onion.

Buttered Noodles

3 qts. water
1 tablespoon salt
3 cups (about 8 oz.) noodles
3 tablespoons melted butter

1. Heat water and salt to boiling in a large saucepan.
2. Add noodles gradually.
3. Boil rapidly, uncovered, 6 to 10 min., or until tender. Test tenderness by pressing a piece against side of pan with fork or spoon.
4. Drain noodles by turning them into a colander or large sieve; rinse with hot water to remove loose starch. Turn noodles into a warm serving dish. Using a fork, blend butter through noodles.

6 servings

Noodles with Bread Crumbs: Prepare 1 cup **buttered bread crumbs.** Turn noodles into a warm serving dish and sprinkle with crumbs.

Macaroni: Substitute 2 cups (8-oz. pkg.) uncooked **macaroni** (tubes broken into 1- to 2-in. pieces, elbows or other shapes) for the noodles. Boil 10 to 15 min. Continue as in recipe.

Shrimp, Viennese-Style

- **2 lbs. fresh shrimp with shells**
- **1 qt. water**
- **¼ cup lemon juice**
- **1 tablespoon salt**
- **1 bay leaf**
- **¼ cup butter**
- **2 tablespoons chopped green onion**
- **½ cup white wine**
- **1 tablespoon tomato paste**
- **¼ teaspoon sugar**
- **½ teaspoon salt**
- **Few grains cayenne pepper**
- **1 tablespoon butter**
- **1 tablespoon all-purpose flour**

1. *To Cook Shrimp*—Wash shrimp with shells in cold water.
2. Drop shrimp into a boiling mixture of water, lemon juice, 1 tablespoon salt and bay leaf.
3. Cover tightly. Simmer 5 min., or until shrimp are pink and tender. Drain and cover with cold water to chill. Drain shrimp again. Remove tiny legs and peel shells from shrimp. Cut a slit to just below surface along back (outer curved surface) of shrimp to expose the black vein. With knife point, remove vein in one piece. Rinse shrimp quickly in cold water. Drain on absorbent paper.
4. *To Complete*—Heat ¼ cup butter in a skillet.
5. Add the shrimp and onion.
6. Cook over medium heat about 3 min.
7. Remove from heat and blend in a mixture of wine, tomato paste, sugar, ½ teaspoon salt, and pepper.
8. Return to heat and simmer 15 min. Remove the shrimp and set aside.
9. Heat 1 tablespoon butter in a saucepan.
10. Blend in flour.
11. Heat until mixture bubbles. Remove from heat. Add gradually 3 tablespoons of the shrimp sauce, stirring constantly. Immediately blend into the sauce in the skillet. Bring to boiling. Cook 1 to 2 min.
12. Add the shrimp and cook over medium heat 5 min., or until thoroughly heated. Serve hot.

6 servings

Potato Pancakes

- **2 tablespoons all-purpose flour**
- **1½ teaspoons salt**
- **¼ teaspoon baking powder**
- **⅛ teaspoon pepper**
- **6 medium-size (about 2 lbs.) potatoes (about 3 cups, grated)**
- **Fat (enough to make a layer ¼ in. deep)**
- **2 eggs, well beaten**
- **1 tablespoon grated onion**
- **1 tablespoon minced parsley**

1. Combine flour, salt, baking powder, and pepper. Set aside.
2. Wash, pare and finely grate potatoes. Set aside.
3. Heat fat in a heavy skillet over low heat.
4. Combine the flour mixture with eggs, onion and parsley.
5. Drain liquid that collects from grated potatoes; add potatoes to egg mixture and beat thoroughly with a spoon.
6. When fat is hot, spoon about 2 tablespoons of batter for each pancake into fat, leaving about 1 in. between pancakes. Cook over medium heat until golden brown and crisp on one side. Turn carefully and brown other side. Drain on absorbent paper.
7. Serve with **Sauerbraten** or as a main dish accompanied by **apple sauce.**

About 20 medium-size pancakes

Potato Pancakes, King-Size: Use a large, heavy skillet. Heat 2 tablespoons **fat** in the skillet. Spoon about one-third of batter into skillet. Quickly spread batter evenly with spoon to cover bottom, making one large pancake. When golden brown and crisp, turn carefully. Add 2 tablespoons **shortening** and brown other side. Repeat for rest of batter.

3 large pancakes

Medium White Sauce

2 tablespoons butter
2 tablespoons all-purpose flour
¼ teaspoon salt
Few grains pepper
1 cup milk

1. Heat butter in a saucepan over low heat.
2. Blend in flour, salt and pepper.
3. Heat until mixture bubbles. Remove from heat.
4. Add milk gradually, stirring well.
5. Cook rapidly, stirring constantly, until sauce thickens. Cook 1 to 2 min. longer.

About 1 cup sauce

Thin White Sauce: Use 1 tablespoon **butter** and 1 tablespoon **flour.**

Mushroom Sauce: Clean and slice ½ cup **mushrooms.** Heat 1 tablespoon **butter** in a skillet. Add the mushrooms and cook until lightly browned and tender. Mix into the cooked white sauce.

Onion Sauce

2 cups Quick Meat Broth (page 9)
½ cup butter
¼ cup chopped onion
3 tablespoons (about 1 small) chopped carrot
1 bay leaf
4½ tablespoons all-purpose flour

1. Prepare broth and set aside.
2. Melt butter in a skillet. Add and cook about 5 min., onion, carrot and bay leaf.
3. Blend flour into mixture in skillet.
4. Heat until mixture bubbles, stirring constantly. Remove from heat. Gradually add the meat broth while stirring constantly. Return to heat and bring rapidly to boiling, stirring constantly; cook 1 to 2 min. longer. Remove bay leaf.

About 2 cups sauce

Mushroom-Onion Sauce: Omit carrot. Clean and slice ½ cup **mushrooms.** Add with the onion to butter in skillet; cook until onion and mushrooms are lightly browned and tender, occasionally moving and turning with a spoon. After mushrooms are browned, remove with a slotted spoon and set aside. Return to skillet after sauce has thickened. Heat thoroughly.

Vegetables

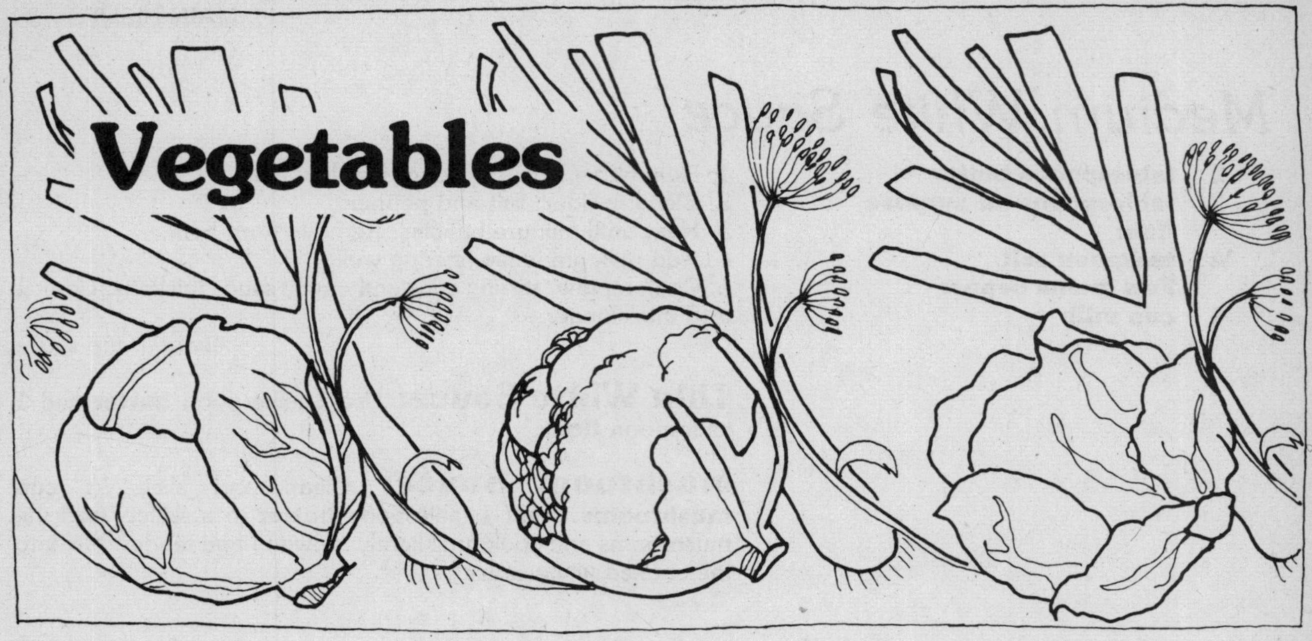

Probably the most popular of all German vegetables are potatoes and cabbage. The cabbage is usually in the form of sauerkraut. This pungent delicacy was created in Germany and has been accepted as part of their national diet by other European countries. Root vegetables, especially potatoes and turnips or rutabagas, and cabbage (both red and white), as well as leeks, snap beans, chives, lettuce, kale and spinach are widely used in Central Europe and are the basis for many tasty dishes. Along with the sweet-sour flavor, so characteristic of German and Viennese cookery, the enjoyable piquancy of anise, caraway and cardamom seeds are part of the culinary charm. And where rich cream is a popular favorite these cooks use it liberally, either sweet or sour.

How To Cook Vegetables

Wash fresh vegetables, but do not soak them in water for any length of time. If they are wilted, put them in cold water for a few minutes. Cauliflower, broccoli, artichokes and Brussels sprouts are sometimes immersed in cold salted water before they are cooked.

Baking—Bake such vegetables as potatoes, tomatoes and squash without removing skins. Pare vegetables for oven dishes, following directions given with recipes.

Boiling—Have water boiling rapidly before adding vegetables. Add salt at beginning of cooking period (1/4 teaspoon per cup of water). After adding vegetables, again bring water to boiling as quickly as possible. If more water is needed, add boiling water. Boil at a moderate rate and cook vegetables until just tender.

In general, cook vegetables in a covered pan, in the smallest amount of water and for the shortest time possible. Exceptions are:

Aparagus—arranged in tied bundles with stalks standing in bottom of a double boiler containing water to cover lower half of spears—cover with inverted double boiler top.

Broccoli—trimmed of leaves and bottoms of stalks. If stalks are over 1 in. in diameter, make lengthwise gashes through them almost to flowerets. Cook quickly in a covered skillet or saucepan in 1 in. of boiling, salted water 10 to 15 min., or just until tender.

Cabbage (mature)—cooked, loosely covered in just enough water to cover. Cabbage (young)—cooked, tightly covered, in a minimum amount of water (do not overcook).

To restore color to red cabbage, add a small amount of vinegar at end of cooking period, just before draining.

Cauliflower (whole head)—cooked, uncovered, in a 1 in. depth of boiling, salted water for 5 min., then covered, 15 to 20 min.

Mature Root Vegetables (potatoes, rutabagas, parsnips)—cooked, covered, in just enough boiling, salted water to cover vegetables.

Spinach—cooked, covered, with only the water which clings to leaves after final washing.

Broiling—Follow directions in recipes.

Frying and Deep Frying—Follow directions in specific recipes.

Panning—Finely shred or slice vegetables. Cook slowly until just tender in a small amount of fat, in a covered, heavy pan. Occasionally move with a spoon to prevent sticking and burning.

Steaming—Steam mild-flavored vegetables, except those having a green color. Cooking in a pressure saucepan is a form of steaming. Follow directions given with saucepan because overcooking may occur in a matter of seconds.

Note: Some saucepans having tight-fitting covers may lend themselves to steaming vegetables in as little as 1 teaspoon water, no water or a small amount of butter or shortening.

Canned Vegetables—Heat to boiling in liquid from can.

Home Canned Vegetables—Boil 10 min. (not required for tomatoes or sauerkraut).

Dried (dehydrated) Vegetables—Soak and cook as directed in specific recipes.

Frozen Vegetables—Do not thaw before cooking (except thaw corn on cob and partially thaw spinach). Break frozen block apart with fork during cooking. Use as little boiling salted water as possible for cooking. Follow directions on package.

Cauliflower with Mustard Sauce

1 medium-size head cauliflower
1 cup heavy cream
¼ cup sugar
2 tablespoons dry mustard
2 teaspoons cornstarch
½ teaspoon salt
1 egg yolk, slightly beaten
¼ cup cider vinegar

1. *For Cauliflower*—Remove leaves, cut off all the woody base and trim any blemishes from cauliflower.
2. Rinse and cook the cauliflower 20 to 25 min. or until tender but still firm.
3. *For Mustard Sauce*—Meanwhile, set out cream. Scald in top of double boiler ¾ cup of the cream.
4. Sift together into a small saucepan sugar, mustard, cornstarch, and salt.
5. Add, stirring well, the remaining ¼ cup cream. Gradually add the scalded cream; stir constantly. Stirring gently and constantly, bring cornstarch mixture rapidly to boiling over direct heat and cook for 3 min.
6. Wash double-boiler top to remove scum.
7. Pour mixture into double-boiler top and place over simmering water. Cover and cook 10 to 12 min., stirring occasionally. Remove cover and vigorously stir about 3 tablespoons of this hot mixture into egg yolk.
8. Immediately blend into mixture in double boiler. Cook over simmering water 3 to 5 min. Stir slowly to keep mixture cooking evenly. Remove from heat. Add gradually, stirring in vinegar.
9. Drain the cauliflower and serve on platter with **Schnitzel Holstein** or on a separate plate; pour the sauce over cauliflower.

4 servings

Cauliflower a la Mousseline*

1 large head cauliflower
2 egg yolks
2 tablespoons cream
½ teaspoon salt
½ teaspoon sugar
¼ teaspoon paprika
2½ tablespoons lemon juice
¼ cup butter
2 egg whites
Paprika

1. *For Cauliflower*—Remove leaves, cut off all woody base and trim any blemishes from cauliflower.
2. Separate the head into flowerets and cook 8 to 10 min., or until just tender. Drain and set aside to keep warm.
3. *For Sauce*—In the top of a small double boiler, beat with a whisk beater until thickened and light-colored egg yolks and cream.
4. Blend in a mixture of salt, sugar and paprika.
5. Set over hot (not boiling) water; bottom of double-boiler top should not touch water. Add lemon juice gradually, beating constantly.
6. Cook over low heat, beating constantly with the whisk beater, until sauce has the consistency of thick cream. Remove double boiler from heat, leaving top in place. Beating constantly, add butter to egg yolk mixture, ½ teaspoon at a time.
7. Beat with whisk beater until butter is thoroughly blended into the mixture. Remove top of double boilder from bottom.
8. Beat egg whites until rounded peaks are formed.
9. Fold egg whites into the sauce. Arrange cauliflower on platter or in serving dish and spoon sauce over flowerets. Sprinkle with paprika.

6 servings

*True mousseline sauce is made by folding whipped cream into hollandaise sauce; but as here, beaten egg white may be used if preferred.

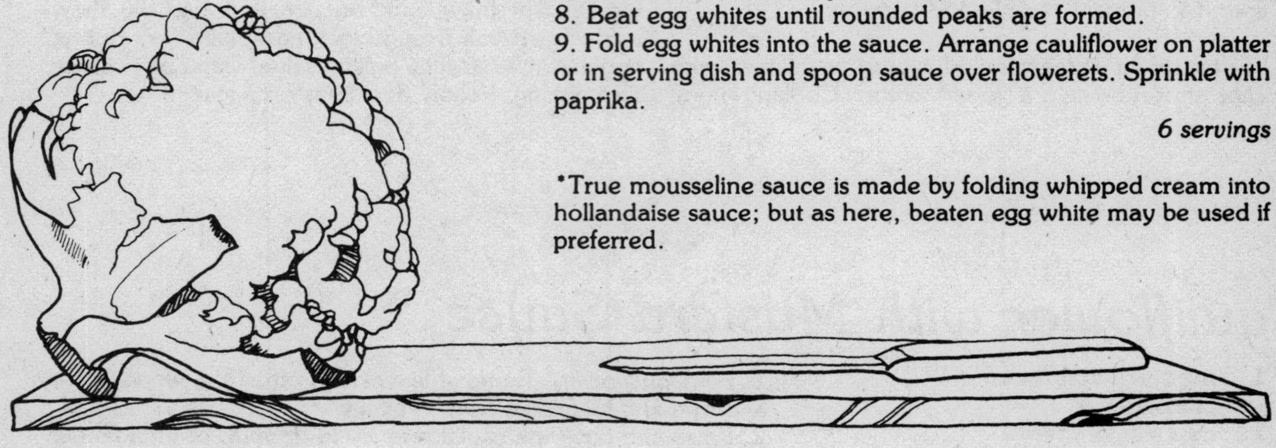

Sweet-Sour Red Cabbage

1 head (about 2 lbs.) red cabbage
Boiling salted water to cover (1 teaspoon salt per quart of water)
½ cup firmly packed brown sugar
¾ teaspoon allspice
4 whole cloves
½ cup vinegar
¼ cup butter

1. Set out a heavy 3-qt. saucepan.
2. Remove and discard wilted outer leaves from cabbage.
3. Rinse, cut into quarters (discarding core) and coarsely shred (about 2 qts., shredded). Put cabbage into the saucepan and add water, sugar, allspice, and cloves.
4. Cover loosely and boil at a moderate rate 8 to 12 min., or until cabbage is just tender.
5. Remove from heat; drain. Add vinegar and butter to cabbage.
6. Toss together lightly to mix.

6 servings

Red Cabbage with Apples: Wash, quarter, core, pare, and chop 3 **apples.** Add to saucepan with cabbage. Cook until apples and cabbage are just tender.

Red Cabbage and Wine

1 head (about 2 lbs.) red cabbage
1 cup red wine
1/3 cup firmly packed brown sugar
1 teaspoon salt
Few grains cayenne pepper
4 medium-size apples
1/4 cup cider vinegar
1/4 cup butter

1. Set out a heavy 3-qt. saucepan having a tight-fitting cover.
2. Remove and discard wilted outer leaves from cabbage.
3. Rinse, cut into quarters (discarding core) and coarsely shred (about 2 qts., shredded). Put cabbage into the saucepan with wine, sugar, salt, and pepper.
4. Rinse, quarter, core and pare apples. Add the apples to the saucepan.
5. Cover and simmer over low heat 20 to 30 min., or until cabbage is tender. Add vinegar and butter to the cabbage. Toss together lightly until butter is melted.

6 servings

Sauerkraut with Caraway Seeds

1 27 oz. can sauerkraut (about 3½ cups, drained)
2 cups boiling water
2 tablespoons butter, melted
½ teaspoon salt
1 teaspoon caraway seeds
1/8 teaspoon pepper

1. Drain contents of can of sauerkraut.
2. Put sauerkraut into a large, heavy saucepan and pour water over it.
3. Cook over low heat about 45 min., or until most of the liquid is absorbed and the sauerkraut is thoroughly heated. Drain the sauerkraut and put into a serving dish.
4. Toss lightly with a mixture of butter, salt, caraway seeds, and pepper.

6 to 8 servings

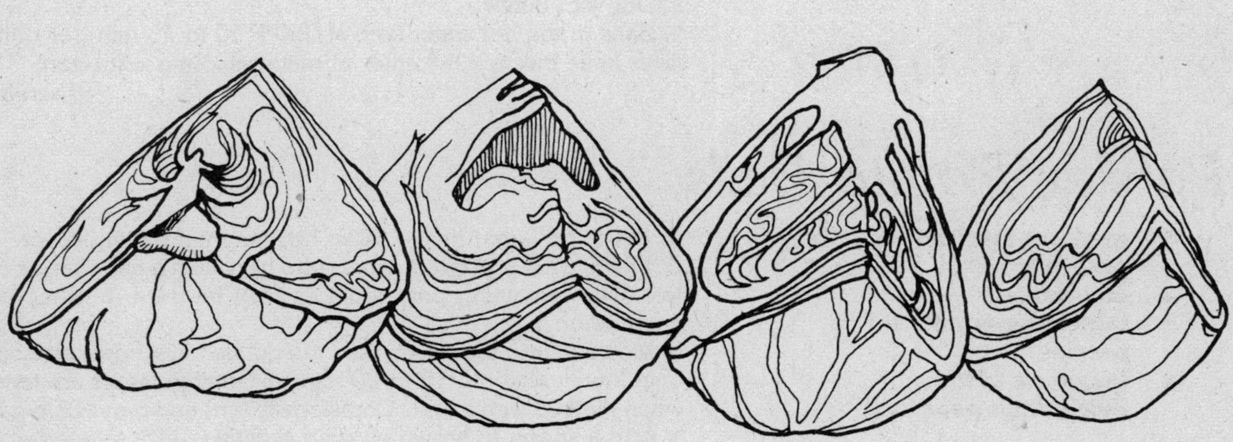

Kohlrabi with Sour Cream

2 lbs. (about 8 medium-size) kohlrabi
3 tablespoons butter
¼ cup hot water
½ teaspoon salt
1 cup thick sour cream
1 tablespoon all-purpose flour
⅛ teaspoon cayenne pepper

1. Set out a large skillet, having a tight-fitting cover.
2. Trim off leaves and stems, wash and pare kohlrabi.
3. Cut into ½-in. cubes. Heat butter in the skillet.
4. Add kohlrabi and cook about 2 min., moving and turning pieces with a spoon; then add hot water and salt.
5. Cover tightly and cook at a moderate rate about 10 min., or until tender. (There should be little or no water at the end of cooking.)
6. Meanwhile, blend together sour cream, flour, and pepper.
7. Push kohlrabi to one side of skillet; add the sour cream mixture gradually to the skillet, stirring constantly. When well blended, stir in the kohlrabi and cook, constantly moving and turning with a spoon, until sauce becomes thicker. Cook 1 to 2 min. longer.

6 servings

Leeks with Sour Cream: Substitute 8 large **leeks** for the kohlrabi. Trim off roots and tough part of green tops. Rinse and peel. Rinse again and cut into ¾-in. slices.

Leeks au Gratin

1 oz. sharp Cheddar cheese (about ¼ cup, grated)
2 lbs. large tender leeks
4 eggs, slightly beaten
3 tablespoons thick sour cream
¼ teaspoon salt
2 tablespoons fine dry bread crumbs (page 8)
2 tablespoons butter

1. Heat the water for hot water bath. Butter a shallow 10x6x2-in. baking dish.
2. Grate cheese and set aside.
3. Trim off roots and tough part of green tops of leeks, rinse and peel.
4. Rinse and cut into lengthwise halves. Put leeks into a saucepan, cover with a large amount of boiling water and cook as for strong-flavored vegetables until tender, about 10 min. Drain thoroughly. Arrange in dish.
5. Beat together just until blended eggs, sour cream, and salt.
6. Pour mixture over leeks. Sprinkle over the top the grated cheese and bread crumbs.
7. Dot with butter.
8. Bake in the hot water bath at 350°F 10 to 15 min., or until a silver knife inserted in center of mixture comes out clean.

5 servings

Parsley Potato Balls

6 medium-size (about 2 lbs.) potatoes
¼ cup butter
2 tablespoons minced parsley
½ teaspoon salt
Few grains paprika

1. Set out a large, heavy skillet having a tight-fitting cover.
2. Wash, pare and cut potatoes into balls with a ball-shaped cutter. (The remaining potato pieces may be used in other food preparation.)
3. Melt butter in the skillet. Add the potato balls, cover and cook over low heat about 15 to 20 min., or until potatoes are tender when pierced with a fork. Occasionally turn and move balls gently with a spoon to brown all sides slightly.
4. Toss potato balls with a mixture of parsley, salt, and paprika.

About 4 servings

Raw-Fried Potatoes

1/3 cup butter
1 large potato
1/4 teaspoon salt

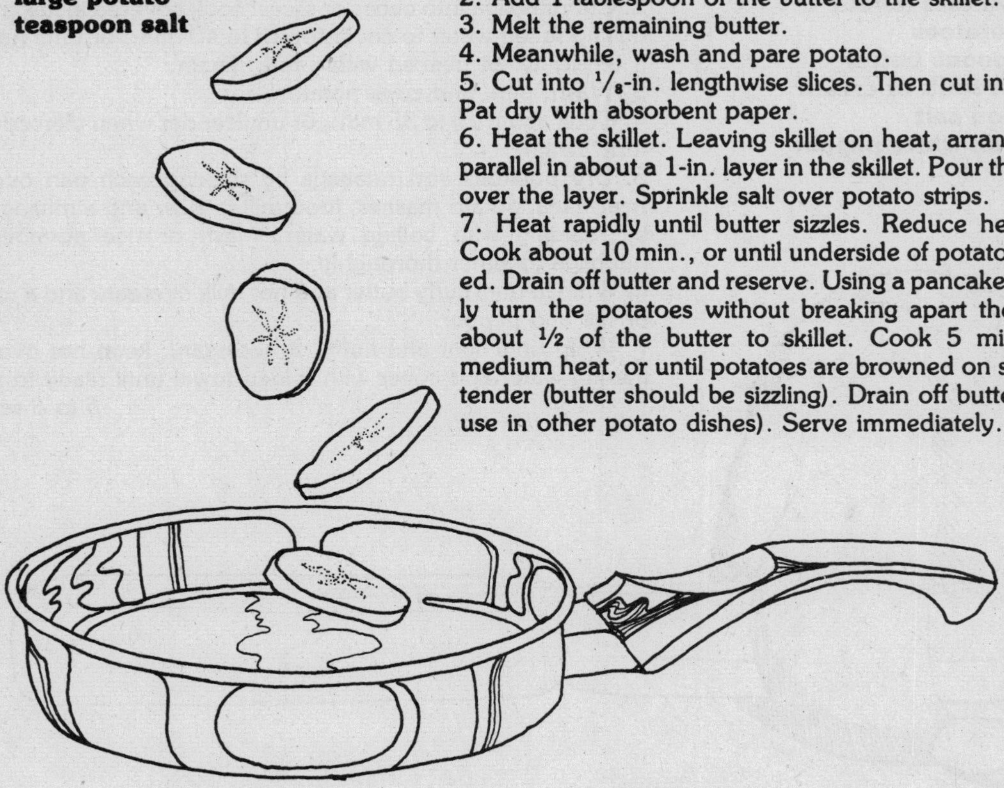

1. Set out a 6-in. skillet and butter.
2. Add 1 tablespoon of the butter to the skillet.
3. Melt the remaining butter.
4. Meanwhile, wash and pare potato.
5. Cut into 1/8-in. lengthwise slices. Then cut into 1/8-in. strips. Pat dry with absorbent paper.
6. Heat the skillet. Leaving skillet on heat, arrange potato strips parallel in about a 1-in. layer in the skillet. Pour the melted butter over the layer. Sprinkle salt over potato strips.
7. Heat rapidly until butter sizzles. Reduce heat to medium. Cook about 10 min., or until underside of potato layer is browned. Drain off butter and reserve. Using a pancake turner, carefully turn the potatoes without breaking apart the layer. Return about 1/2 of the butter to skillet. Cook 5 min. longer over medium heat, or until potatoes are browned on second side and tender (butter should be sizzling). Drain off butter. (Reserve for use in other potato dishes). Serve immediately.

3 to 4 servings

Paprika Potatoes

2 cups Quick Meat Broth (page 9)
6 medium-size (about 2 lbs.) potatoes
2 tablespoons butter
1/4 cup chopped onion
2 tablespoons all-purpose flour
1 teaspoon paprika
1/2 teaspoon salt
1 cup thick sour cream
2 tablespoons tomato paste
Sprigs of parsley

1. Set out a large, heavy skillet.
2. Prepare broth and set aside.
3. Wash and scrub potatoes with a vegetable brush.
4. Cook about 30 min., or until potatoes are tender when pierced with a fork. Drain potatoes. Dry potatoes by shaking pan over low heat. Peel potatoes and cut into cubes.
5. Meanwhile, heat butter in the skillet.
6. Add onion and cook over medium heat until onion is golden yellow in color. Blend in flour, paprika, and salt.
7. Heat until mixture bubbles. Remove from heat. Gradually add the meat broth, stirring constantly. Bring to boiling. Cook 1 to 2 min. Remove skillet from heat. Stirring vigorously with a French whip, whisk beater or fork, add to contents of skillet in very small amounts, a mixture of sour cream and tomato paste.
8. Gently mix potatoes into the sauce and cook over low heat, moving and turning constantly with a spoon, 3 to 5 min., or until thoroughly heated. Do not boil.
9. Turn into a serving dish and garnish with sprigs of parsley. Serve immediately.

6 servings

Whipped Potatoes and Rutabaga

½ lb. rutabaga
4 medium-size (about 1⅓ lbs.) potatoes
2 tablespoons butter
¼ cup hot milk or cream
1 teaspoon salt
⅛ teaspoon white pepper

1. Wash, cut into halves and pare rutabaga.
2. Cut rutabaga into cubes or slices: cook covered in just enough boiling salted water to cover for 25 to 40 min., or until rutabaga is tender when pierced with a fork. Drain.
3. Wash, pare and cook potatoes.
4. Cook about 25 to 35 min., or until tender when pierced with a fork. Drain.
5. Dry potatoes and rutabaga by shaking each pan over low heat. Heat potato masher, food mill or ricer and a mixing bowl, by scalding with boiling water. Mash or rice potatoes and rutabaga together thoroughly.
6. Whip in until fluffy butter and hot milk or cream and a mixture of salt and pepper.
7. Whip until light and fluffy. If necessary, keep hot over simmering water and cover with folded towel until ready to serve.

6 to 8 servings

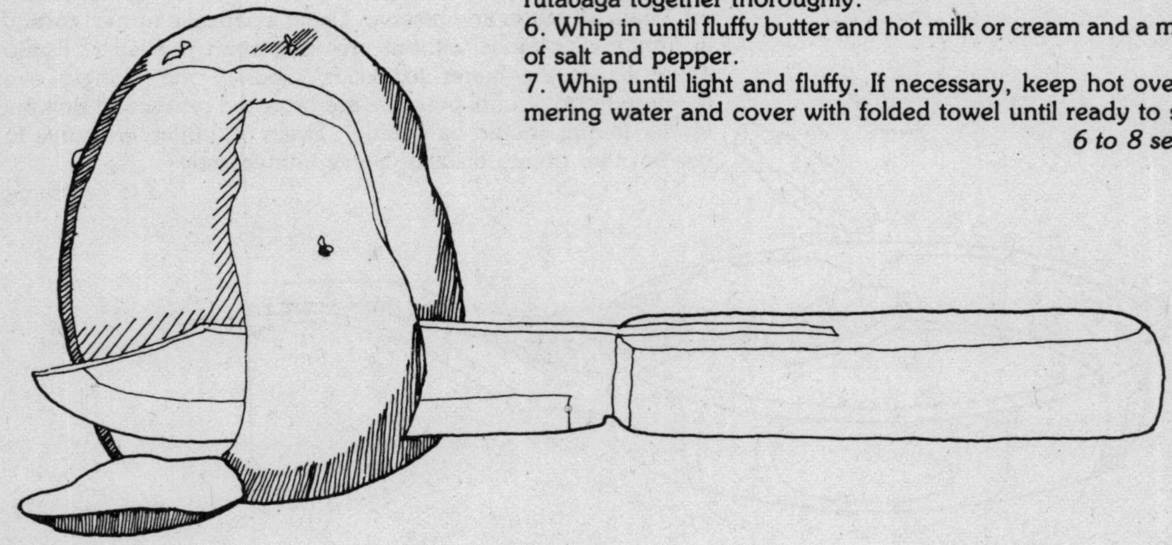

Hot Potato Salad

6 medium-size (about 2 lbs.) potatoes
¼ cup butter
2 tablespoons minced parsley
½ teaspoon salt
Few grains paprika

1. Wash and cut potatoes into halves.
2. Cook about 20 min., or until potatoes are tender when pierced with a fork. Drain potatoes. Dry potatoes by shaking pan over low heat. Peel and cut into ¼-in slices.
3. Meanwhile, dice and panbroil bacon, reserving bacon drippings. Set aside.
4. Clean and chop onions.
5. Put 6 tablespoons of the bacon drippings into a saucepan. Add the onion and cook until it is tender, occasionally moving and turning with a spoon. Stir in vinegar, sugar, salt, and pepper.
6. Heat mixture to boiling. Add the diced bacon to the onion-vinegar mixture. Pour over the hot potato slices and toss lightly to coat evenly.

Note: To prepare thuringer sausage links, cook covered, in water to cover, about 15 min. over medium heat.

Boiled Potatoes: Cook potatoes. Peel potatoes or serve in jackets. Do not cut into halves or slices.

Cucumber Salad with Sour Cream

1 egg
1 large cucumber
½ cup thick sour cream
1½ tablespoons vinegar
1 tablespoon chopped chives
¾ teaspoon salt
⅛ teaspoon white pepper

1. Hard-cook egg and set aside.
2. Rinse and pare cucumber.
3. Score cucumber ⅛ in. deep by pulling the tines of a fork lengthwise; repeat to score entire surface. Cut cucumber into thin slices. Put into a bowl.
4. Mix sour cream, vinegar, chives, salt, and pepper together.
5. Pour the mixture over the cucumber slices and toss lightly to coat evenly. Chill in refrigerator.
6. When ready to serve, cut the peeled egg into halves, remove egg yolk and chop finely. (The egg white may be used in other food preparation.) Garnish salad with the chopped yolk.

4 to 6 servings

Green Bean Salad

1 lb. green beans
2 small onions
6 slices bacon
⅓ cup vinegar
2½ tablespoons sugar
½ teaspoon salt

1. Wash, cut off and discard ends from beans and cut into 1-in. pieces.
2. Cook 15 to 20 min., or until beans are tender. Drain thoroughly if necessary, and put beans into a bowl. Keep beans warm.
3. Meanwhile clean and cut onions into slices ⅛ in. thick.
4. Separate onion slices into rings and put into bowl with beans.
5. Dice and fry bacon until crisp, without pouring off drippings.
6. Add vinegar, sugar, and salt to skillet containing bacon.
7. Heat mixture to boiling, stirring well. Pour vinegar mixture over beans and onions and toss lightly to coat thoroughly.

4 servings

Wax Bean Salad: Substitute **wax beans** for the green beans.

Quick Pickled Beets

1 16-oz. can sliced beets or small whole beets (about 2 cups, drained)
2 medium-size onions
1 cup vinegar
½ cup sugar
½ teaspoon salt

1. Drain contents of can of sliced beets or small whole beets.
2. Clean onions, slice very thinly and separate into rings.
3. Lightly mix the beets and onions. Set aside.
4. Mix together in a saucepan vinegar, sugar, and salt.
5. Bring to boiling; pour over beets and onions. Cool; chill in refrigerator 1 hr. or longer.

About 6 servings

Cauliflower Salad

- **1 medium-size head cauliflower**
- **1 5-oz. can shrimp**
- **¼ cup vinegar**
- **3 tablespoons salad oil**
- **½ teaspoon salt**
- **⅛ teaspoon white pepper**
- **1 tablespoon chopped parsley**

1. Remove leaves, cut off all the woody base and trim any blemishes from cauliflower
2. Separate the cauliflower into flowerets; rinse and cook 8 to 10 min., or until tender but still firm. Drain the flowerets and set aside to cool. Chill in refrigerator.
3. Meanwhile, drain contents of can of shrimp.
4. Cut the shrimp into pieces and put into a bowl; chill in refrigerator.
5. Combine vinegar, salad oil, salt, and pepper in a screw-top jar.
6. Shake dressing thoroughly and put in refrigerator to chill.
7. When ready to serve, put the chilled caluliflower into a bowl with the chilled shrimp and parsley.
8. Shake the dressing well and pour over the cauliflower. Toss lightly to coat evenly. Serve immediately.

6 servings

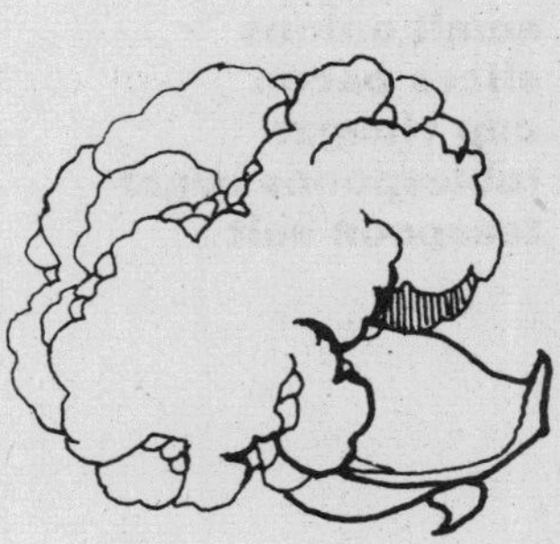

Wilted Lettuce Salad

- **1 small head lettuce**
- **1 egg**
- **¼ cup cider vinegar**
- **¼ cup salad oil**
- **2 tablespoons sugar**
- **½ teaspoon salt**
- **⅛ teaspoon pepper**

1. Using a sharp-pointed knife, remove core from lettuce.
2. Rinse with cold water and drain well. Gently pat dry. Tear lettuce into pieces. Put into a bowl. Cover and chill in refrigerator.
3. Hard-cook egg and peel.
4. Cut egg into slices crosswise and set aside.
5. Combine in a small skillet vinegar, oil, sugar, salt, and pepper.
6. Heat mixture to boiling, stirring well. Immediately pour vinegar mixture over the lettuce and toss lightly to coat lettuce thoroughly.
7. Garnish with the hard-cooked egg slices.

6 servings

Wilted Lettuce with Bacon: The egg may be omitted. Dice 6 slices **bacon;** fry until crisp without pouring off fat. Substitute the **bacon fat** for the salad oil. Omit salt and pepper.

Mustard Relish Mold

- **1 cup cold water**
- **2 env. unflavored gelatin**
- **6 eggs**
- **1½ cups sugar**
- **1½ tablespoons dry mustard**
- **1¼ teaspoons salt**
- **1½ cups vinegar**
- **1 16-oz. can peas (about 1¾ cups, drained)**
- **1 cup (about 2 medium-size) grated carrot**
- **1 cup chopped celery**
- **1 tablespoon minced parsley**
- **Curly endive or other crisp greens**

1. A 1½-qt. mold will be needed.
2. Pour water into a small bowl.
3. Sprinkle gelatin evenly over cold water.
4. Let stand until softened.
5. Beat eggs slightly in top of a double boiler.
6. Blend in a mixture of sugar, mustard, and salt.
7. Add vinegar gradually, stirring constantly.
8. Cook over simmering water, stirring constantly, until mixture thickens. Remove from simmering water. Stir softened gelatin; add to egg mixture and stir until gelatin is completely dissolved. Cool; chill until mixture begins to gel (gets slightly thicker).
9. Meanwhile drain contents of 1 16-oz. can peas.
10. Lightly oil the mold with salad or cooking oil (not olive oil) and set it aside to drain.
11. Prepare carrot, celery, and parsley.
12. When gelatin is of desired consistency, blend in the vegetables. Turn into the prepared mold. Chill in refrigerator until firm.
13. Unmold onto chilled serving plate. Garnish with curly endive or other crisp greens.

About 12 servings

Kraut with Apples

- **4 cups drained sauerkraut**
- **2 apples, thinly sliced**
- **½ cup apple cider**
- **1 tablespoon light brown sugar**
- **2 tablespoons butter or margarine**

Mix all ingredients. Cover and simmer 5 minutes, or until apples are tender. Garnish with *apple wedges* and *parsley*.

About 8 servings

German Potato Salad

- **12 slices bacon, diced and fried until crisp (reserve 6 tablespoons drippings)**
- **3 medium-sized onions, chopped (2 cups)**
- **1 cup less 2 tablespoons cider vinegar**
- **1½ tablespoons sugar**
- **1½ teaspoons salt**
- **¼ teaspoon pepper**
- **2- 3 lbs. potatoes, cooked, peeled, and cut in ¼-inch slices**

1. Heat bacon drippings in a skillet. Add onion and cook until tender, stirring occasionally. Stir in vinegar, sugar, salt, and pepper; heat to boiling. Mix in bacon.
2. Pour over potato slices in a serving dish and toss lightly to coat evenly. Garnish with snipped parsley and paprika. Serve hot.

About 6 servings

Dumplings

Central Europe is the home of the dumpling and all its numerous family. In no other part of the world does a bit of dough or batter do so much for so many and in so many different ways. Dumplings are cooked in soups, steamed or cooked in boiling water for main-dish accompaniments, wrapped around fresh fruits for desserts. They may be made from flour or from grated potato or from cereals, of quick-bread dough or raised dough. They come in all sizes and may have blended into them, depending on their function in the meal, all sorts of seasonings. Sometimes texture contrast is supplied by adding croutons.

Fish Dumplings

2 qts. water
1 teaspoon salt
2 cups (3 slices) soft bread crumbs
1 egg, well beaten
¼ cup milk
1 lb. fish fillets (sole, cod or trout)
1 tablespoon butter
3 tablespoons chopped onion
2 tablespoons grated Parmesan cheese
1 teaspoon finely chopped parsley
1 teaspoon salt
¼ teaspoon white pepper
¼ cup all-purpose flour
Mushroom sauce (page 39)

1. Bring water and 1 teaspoon salt to boiling in a large, heavy saucepan.
2. Put bread crumbs, egg, and milk into a large bowl, blend thoroughly and set aside.
3. Wipe fillets with a clean, damp cloth. (If frozen, thaw according to directions on package.) Force through the medium blade of a food chopper.
4. Heat butter in a skillet.
5. Add onion and cook over medium heat until onion is tender.
6. Add the fish and the contents of the skillet to the bread crumb mixture with cheese, parsley, salt, and pepper.
7. Shape pieces of the fish mixture into balls about 1½ in. in diameter. Roll lightly in flour.
8. Drop the dumplings into the boiling salted water. Cook only as many dumplings at one time as will lie uncrowded one layer deep. Cook about 6 min., or until dumplings rise to the surface of the water. Remove with a slotted spoon and drain over the water for a few seconds. Serve immediately with mushroom sauce.

12 dumplings

Plain Dumplings

- **1 qt. Quick Meat Broth or Quick Chicken Broth (page 9)**
- **2 cups sifted all-purpose flour**
- **4 teaspoons baking powder**
- **1 teaspoon salt**
- **1 tablespoon shortening**
- **⅔ cup milk**
- **1 tablespoon chopped parsley**

1. Prepare Meat Broth or Chicken Broth in a deep saucepan having a tight-fitting cover.
2. Sift together flour, baking powder, and salt.
3. Cut in shortening with a pastry blender or two knives until pieces are the size of rice kernels.
4. Quickly stir in milk and parsley with a fork until just blended.
5. Shape dough into balls about 2 in. in diameter.
6. Bring broth to boiling. Drop dumplings into the broth. Cook only as many dumplings at one time as will lie uncrowded one layer deep. Cover and simmer 15 min. without removing the cover.
7. Carefully remove with a slotted spoon and serve with meat or poultry. (If desired, dumplings may be dropped into boiling soup. Serve the dumplings with the soup.)

12 dumplings

Plain Dumplings with Bacon: Dice and pan-broil 6 slices **bacon;** stir in with the milk.

Herb Dumplings: Add 1 teaspoon marjoram to dry ingredients.

Potato Dumplings

- **6 medium-size (about 2 lbs.) potatoes**
- **1½ tablespoons butter**
- **1 slice toasted bread**
- **2 qts. water**
- **2 teaspoons salt**
- **1 egg, well beaten**
- **1 teaspoon salt**
- **⅛ white pepper**
- **⅔ cup sifted all-purpose flour**
- **¼ cup cornstarch**
- **Melted butter**

1. Wash, pare and cook potatoes.
2. Cook about 30 min., or until potatoes are tender when pierced with a fork. Drain.
3. Dry potatoes by shaking pan over low heat. Mash or rice potatoes thoroughly. Set aside to cool completely.
4. Meanwhile, melt butter in a large, heavy skillet over low heat.
5. Cut bread into ¼- to ½-in. cubes.
6. Put cubes into the skillet and toss until all sides are coated and browned. Set aside.
7. Bring water and salt to boiling in a large, heavy saucepan.
8. When potatoes are cooled, whip egg in until fluffy and a mixture of 1 teaspoon salt, and pepper.
9. Measure flour and cornstarch.
10. Add the cornstarch and one-half the flour. Add enough of the remaining flour to make a soft dough. Break off pieces of the dough and shape into balls about 1 in. in diameter. Poke one of the bread cubes into the center of each ball.
11. Drop the dumplings into the boiling water. Cook only as many dumplings at one time as will lie uncrowded one layer deep. Cook about 5 min., or until dumplings rise to the surface of the water. Carefully remove with a slotted spoon and drain over the water a few seconds.
12. Put dumplings into a warm serving dish and serve with melted butter. Dumplings may be served with sauerkraut, meat or poultry.

About 18 dumplings

Drop Noodles

2 qts. water
2 teaspoons salt
2⅓ cups sifted all-purpose flour
1 teaspoon salt
1 egg, slightly beaten
1 cup water
¼ cup butter, melted

1. Bring to boiling in a 3- or 4-qt. saucepan 2 qts. water and 2 teaspoons salt.
2. Meanwhile, sift together and set aside flour and 1 teaspoon salt.
3. Combine in a bowl and mix together egg and 1 cup water.
4. Gradually add flour mixture to egg mixture, stirring until smooth. (Batter should be very thick and break from a spoon instead of pouring in a continous stream.) Spoon batter into the boiling water by ½ teaspoonfuls, dipping spoon into water each time. Cook only one layer of noodles at one time; do not crowd. After noodles rise to the surface, boil gently 5 to 8 min., or until tender when pressed against side of pan with spoon. Remove from water with slotted spoon, draining over water for a second, and place in a warm bowl.
5. Toss butter lightly with noodles. Serve hot.

About 5 cups noodles

Steamed Sweet Dumplings

½ cup milk
½ pkg. (1 teaspoon) active dry yeast
2 tablespoons warm water, 110°F to 115°F (Or if using compressed yeast, soften ½ cake in 2 tablespoons lukewarm water, 80°F to 85°F.)
¼ cup butter
⅓ cup sugar
¼ teaspoon salt
1 cup sifted all-purpose flour
2½ cups sifted all-purpose flour
2 eggs, well beaten
¼ cup white wine
1½ cups milk
1 tablespoon butter
1 tablespoon sugar
Cherry Sauce or Wine Sauce (on this page)

1. Set out a heavy 10-in. skillet having a tight-fitting cover.
2. Scald milk.
3. Meanwhile, soften yeast in water.
4. Set aside.
5. Put butter, sugar, and salt into a large bowl.
6. Immediately pour scalded milk over ingredients in bowl. When lukewarm, blend in flour, beating until smooth.
7. Stir softened yeast and add, mixing well.
8. Measure 2 to 2½ cups of flour.
9. Add about one-half the flour to the yeast mixture and beat until very smooth. Beat in eggs.
10. Then beat in enough of the remaining flour to make a soft dough. Turn dough onto a lightly floured surface and let rest 5 to 10 min.
11. Knead. Form dough into a large ball and place in a greased bowl. Turn dough to bring greased surface to top. Cover with waxed paper and a towel and let stand in warm place (about 80°) until dough is doubled.
12. Punch down and turn dough out onto lightly floured surface. Shape dough into balls about 1 in. in diameter. Cover with waxed paper and a towel and let rise on rolling surface until balls are doubled.
13. Put milk, butter, and sugar into the skillet.
14. Put about eight of the balls into the skillet. Do not set them too close together. Cover and cook over high heat until steam appears. Reduce heat and cook 30 min., or until steaming stops. Do not remove cover during cooking! Carefully remove dumplings with a slotted spoon to serving dishes and serve with **Cherry Sauce** or **Wine Sauce.**

About 24 dumplings

Cottage Cheese Plum Dumplings

- **½ lb. (about 1 cup, firmly packed) dry cottage cheese**
- **1 cup sifted all-purpose flour**
- **¼ teaspoon salt**
- **3 cups (4 to 5 slices) soft bread crumbs**
- **2 tablespoons butter**
- **2 eggs, well beaten**
- **4 small blue plums**
- **4 cubes of loaf sugar**
- **2 qts. water**
- **Vanilla Sauce (page 53)**

1. Force cottage cheese through a food mill or sieve into a bowl.
2. Sift together and set aside flour and salt.
3. Prepare bread and set aside.
4. Cream butter until softened.
5. Add eggs in thirds, beating well after each addition.
6. Blend in the cottage cheese and the bread crumbs. Add the dry ingredients, beating thoroughly. Set in refrigerator 1 hr.
7. Meanwhile, rinse, cut almost into halves and remove pits from plums.
8. Set out sugar.
9. Insert one of the cubes of sugar into each plum.
10. When dough is chilled, divide into four portions. Shape one portion of the dough around each plum, being sure the plum is completely sealed in.
11. Heat water to boiling in a large, heavy saucepan.
12. Carefully drop the dumplings into the boiling water. Cook about 10 min., or until dumplings rise to the surface. Remove carefully with a slotted spoon and serve with Vanilla Sauce.

4 servings

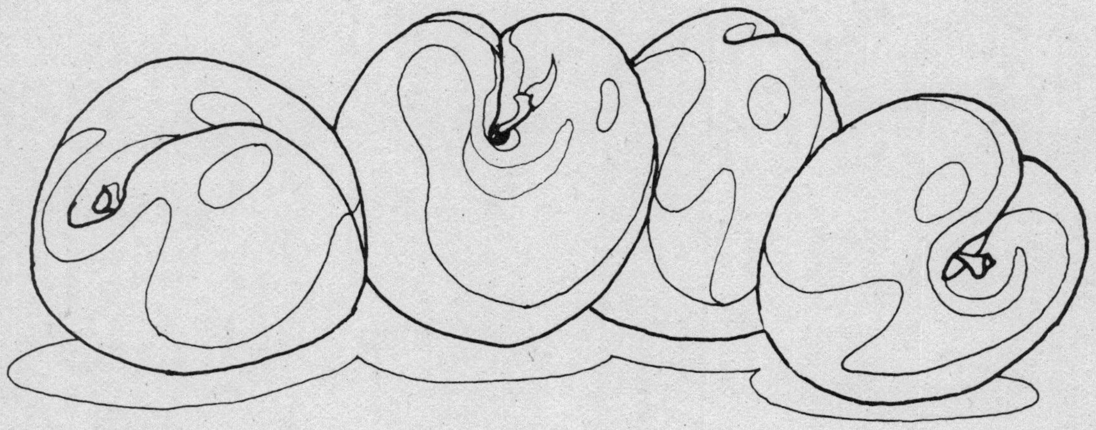

Vanilla Sauce

- **1 cup sugar**
- **2 tablespoons cornstarch**
- **¼ teaspoon salt**
- **2 cups boiling water**
- **1 egg yolk, slightly beaten**
- **¼ cup butter**
- **2 teaspoons vanilla extract**
- **¼ teaspoon nutmeg**

1. Sift sugar, cornstarch, and salt together into the top of a double boiler.
2. Add water, stirring well.
3. Stirring gently and constantly, bring mixture rapidly to boiling over direct heat and cook for 3 min. Place over simmering water. Cover and cook about 12 min., stirring three or four times. Vigorously stir about 3 tablespoons of the hot mixture into egg yolk.
4. Immediately blend into mixture in double boiler. Cook over simmering water 3 to 5 min. Stir slowly to keep mixture cooking evenly. Remove from heat and blend in butter, vanilla extract and nutmeg.

About 2 cups sauce

Wine Sauce: Omit nutmeg. Cool sauce and add gradually, stirring in, ½ cup **white wine.**

Cherry Sauce

2 cups (16-oz. can) pitted red tart cherries
2 whole cloves
2-in. piece stick cinnamon
4 teaspoons sugar
4 teaspoons cornstarch
¼ teaspoon salt
4 teaspoons cold water
3½ tablespoons corn syrup
4 teaspoons butter
1½ teaspoons lemon juice
¼ teaspoon almond extract
1 drop red food coloring
Steamed Sweet Dumplings

1. Cook cherries, cloves, and cinnamon 5 min. in a covered saucepan.
2. Remove from heat; take out and discard cinnamon and cloves. Pour through a sieve or food mill placed over a saucepan. Force cherries through and set aside.
3. Mix sugar, cornstarch, and salt thoroughly in a small bowl.
4. Stir in water and corn syrup, in order, until mixture is smooth.
5. Add gradually, stirring into hot cherry mixture. Bring rapidly to boiling, stirring gently 3 min.
6. Remove from heat and blend in butter, lemon juice, almond extract and red food coloring.

Serve hot with **Steamed Sweet Dumplings.**

About 1½ cups sauce

Desserts

Every person in Central Europe seems to be born with at least one very sweet tooth, and to satisfy it German and Austrian homemakers have developed an astonishing variety of rich desserts. Tortes and strudels abound in both countries. Whipped cream, flavored with liqueur or other essence, is a popular dessert in Vienna. Even desserts that require only the simplest ingredients acquire distinction when prepared in the German and Viennese manner.

Meringue Torte

6 egg whites
2 teaspoons vinegar
1 teaspoon vanilla extract
½ teaspoon almond extract
¼ teaspoon salt
2 cups sugar
Sweetened Whipped Cream (three-fourths recipe, page 62)

1. Grease bottoms only of two 9-in. round layer cake pans with removable bottoms, or line two 9-in. round layer cake pans with unglazed paper cut to fit pan bottoms.
2. Beat egg whites until frothy.
3. Add vinegar, vanilla extract, almond extract, and salt and beat slightly.
4. Add about 2 tablespoons sugar at a time, beating well after each addition.
5. Continue beating until very stiff peaks are formed. Turn equal amounts of meringue into the pans and spread evenly to edges.
6. Bake at 300°F 40 min. Turn off oven and open oven door about 1 or 2 in. Allow torte layers to dry out in oven 30 min. with door partially open. Completely cool torte layers on cooling racks before removing from pans. Remove from pans as directed for torte layers. (It is likely that top surface may become slightly cracked when torte is being removed from pans.)
7. Just before serving, prepare Sweetened Whipped Cream (three-fourths recipe. (If desired, sweetened berries or other fruit may be folded into the whipped cream.) Place one torte layer on a serving plate. Spread the whipped cream evenly over it. Top with second torte layer. Fresh berries arranged on the plate around the torte make an attractive dessert.

12 servings

Blitz Torte

- **Creamy Vanilla Filling (page 61)**
- **½ cup (about 3 oz.) blanched slivered almonds**
- **1 tablespoon sugar**
- **½ teaspoon cinnamon**
- **1 cup sifted cake flour**
- **1 teaspoon baking powder**
- **⅛ teaspoon salt**
- **½ cup butter**
- **1 teaspoon vanilla extract**
- **½ cup sugar**
- **4 egg yolks, well beaten**
- **3 tablespoons milk**
- **4 egg whites**
- **¾ cup sugar**

1. Prepare two 8-in. round layer cake pans.
2. Prepare and chill **Creamy Vanilla Filling.**
3. Prepare almonds and set aside.
4. Mix together sugar and cinnamon and set aside.
5. Sift together flour, baking powder. and salt and set aside.
6. Cream together butter and vanilla extract until softened.
7. Add ½ cup sugar gradually, creaming until fluffy after each addition.
8. Add egg yolk in thirds, beating well after each addition.
9. Measure milk.
10. Mixing only until well blended after each addition, alternately add dry ingredients and milk to creamed mixture, beginning and ending with dry ingredients.
11. Turn batter into pans, spreading to edges.
12. Beat egg whites until frothy.
13. Add ¾ cup sugar, 2 tablespoons at a time, beating well after each addition.
14. Continue beating until very stiff peaks are formed. Carefully spread one-half of meringue over batter in each pan. Sprinkle each layer with half of the slivered almonds and half of the sugar-cinnamon mixture.
15. Bake at 325° 1 hr., or until meringue is delicately browned. Cool torte layers in pans on cooling racks.
16. After cooling, loosen sides with a spatula. Remove one torte layer from pan, peel off waxed paper and place layer, meringue side up, on a serving plate. Spread with all the filling. Remove second layer from pan, peel off waxed paper and place, meringue side up, on top of filling.

About 10 servings

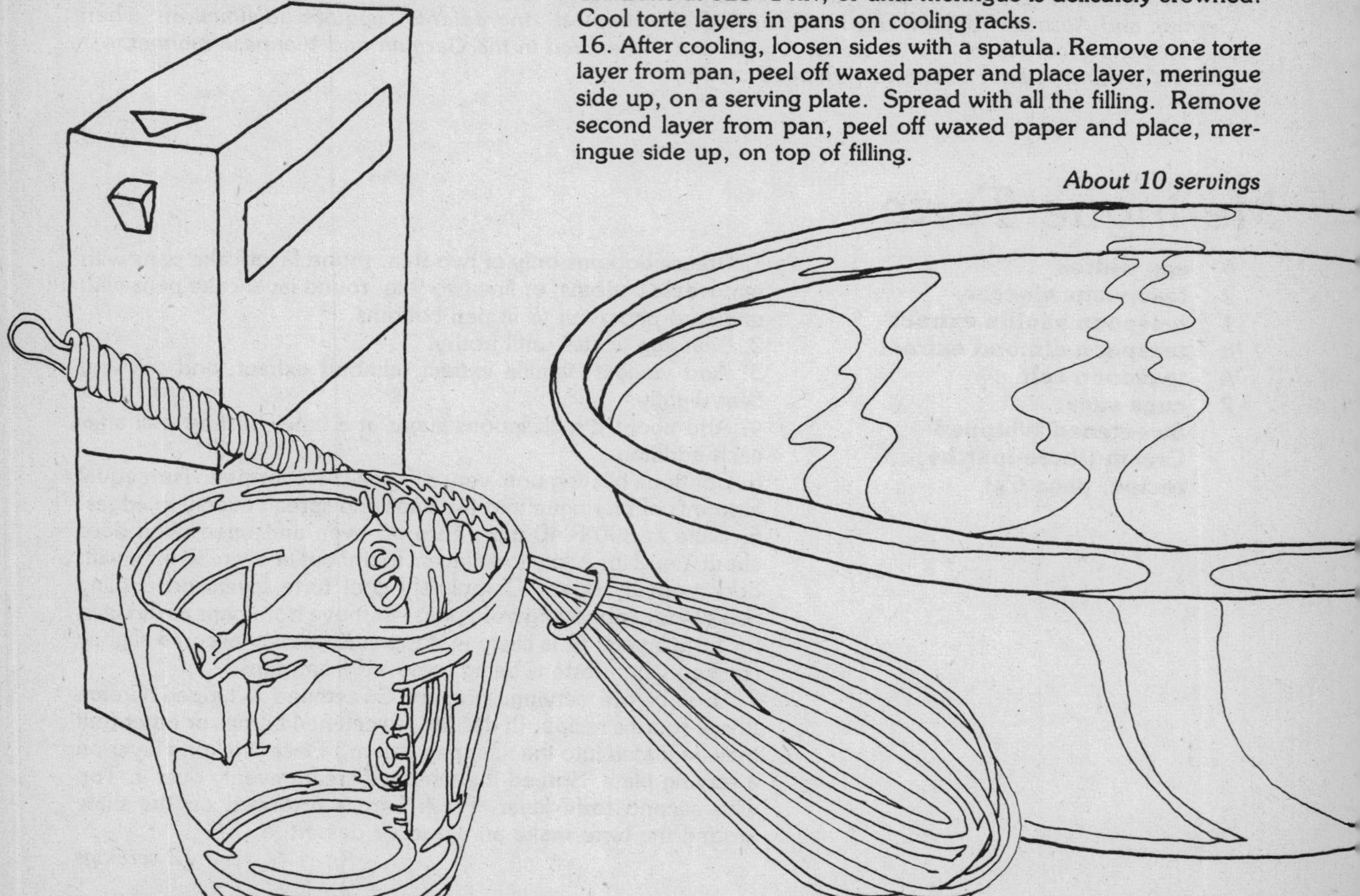

Hazelnut Torte

- **1½ cups (about ½ lb.) hazelnuts (about 4⅓ cups, grated)**
- **½ cup sifted all-purpose flour**
- **½ teaspoon concentrated soluble coffee**
- **½ teaspoon cocoa or Dutch process cocoa**
- **6 egg yolks**
- **½ cup sugar**
- **1 teaspoon grated lemon peel**
- **1 teaspoon rum**
- **½ teaspoon vanilla extract**
- **6 egg whites**
- **¼ teaspoon salt**
- **½ cup sugar**

Hazelnut Butter-Cream Frosting (page 60)

1. Grease bottoms of two 9-in. round layer cake pans with removable bottoms or prepare two 9-in. round layer cake pans.
2. Grate hazelnuts.
3. Sift flour, coffee, and cocoa together.
4. Thoroughly blend hazelnuts with flour mixture. Turn onto a piece of waxed paper and with a spatula mark into four portions; set aside.
5. Combine and beat until very thick and lemon-colored, egg yolks, ½ cup sugar, lemon peel, rum, and vanilla extract. Set egg-yolk mixture aside.
6. Using clean beater, beat egg whites and salt until frothy.
7. Add ½ cup sugar gradually to egg whites, beating well after each addition.
8. Beat the meringue until very stiff peaks are formed.
9. Gently spread egg-yolk mixture over beaten egg whites. Spoon one portion of the flour-hazelnut mixture over egg mixture and gently fold with a few strokes until batter is only *partially* blended. Repeat with second and then third portions. Spoon remaining mixture over batter and gently fold *just* until blended. *Do not overmix!* Gently turn batter into pans and spread to edges.
10. Bake at 350°F 25 to 30 min., or until torte layers test done.
11. Cool and remove from pans.
12. When torte is cooled, prepare Hazelnut Butter-Cream Frosting.
13. Cut one of the torte layers into halves forming 2 equal layers. Fill and frost all three torte layers, placing bottom side of split layer next to plate. Put in refrigerator until ready to serve.

12 to 16 servings

Hazelnut Torte a la Glamour: Prepare and split torte layers. Grate ½ cup (about 2½ oz.) **hazelnuts** (about 1½ cups, grated). Set aside. Prepare **Butter-Cream Frosting** (page 60; using 7 egg **yolks,** ¾ cup plus 2 tablespoons **sugar,** ¾ teaspoon **cornstarch,** ¾ cup plus 2 tablespoons **cream,** and 1½ cups **butter).** Remove and reserve 1 cup of the frosting. Blend the grated nuts into the remaining frosting; fill and frost torte layers. Force some of the remaining frosting through a pastry bag and a No. 1 star tube to make a border around outer edge of top layer. Using a No. 26 decorating tube and remaining frosting, pipe a zigzag decoration from center to border; allow one decoration for each serving. Use No. 26 decorating tube to form rosettes around base.

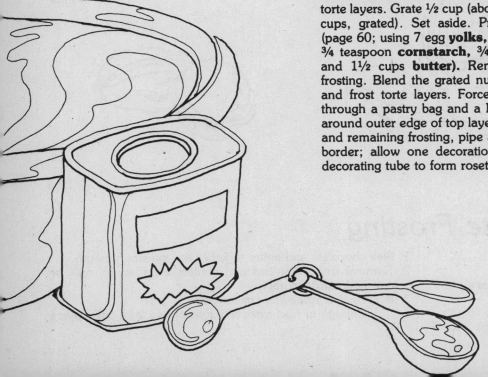

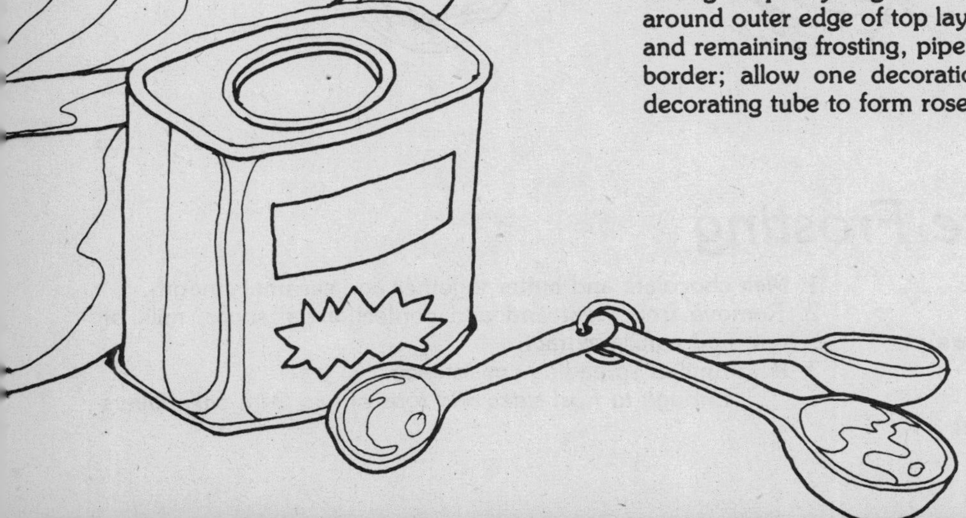

Walnut Torte

- **1** **cup (about 3½ oz.) walnuts (about 1¾ cups, grated)**
- **1** **cup fine, dry bread crumbs (about 3 slices bread)**
- **5** **egg yolks**
- **1** **cup sugar**
- **2** **tablespoons rum**
- **5** **egg whites**
- **Creamy Rum Filling (page 61)**
- **½** **cup (2 oz.) walnuts**

1. Set out a 7-in. spring-form pan.
2. Grate 1 cup (about 3½ oz.) walnuts.
3. Thoroughly mix walnuts with bread crumbs.
4. Turn onto a piece of waxed paper. With a knife divide into four portions and set aside.
5. Beat egg yolks until very thick and lemon-colored.
6. Beat rum in with final few strokes.
7. Set egg yolk mixture aside.
8. Using clean beater, beat egg whites until frothy.
9. Add 2 tablespoons sugar at a time, beating well after each addition.
10. Beat until very stiff peaks are formed. Gently spread egg yolk mixture over beaten egg whites. Spoon one portion of the walnut-bread crumb mixture over egg mixture and gently fold with a few strokes until batter is only *partially* blended. Repeat with second and then third portions of walnut-crumb mixture. Spoon remaining portion over batter and gently fold *just* until blended. *Do not overmix!* Gently turn batter into pan and spread to edges.
11. Bake at 350°F 40 to 45 min., or until torte tests done. Set torte on cooling rack. Cool in pan 15 min. Remove the sides from the bottom of the pan and, if desired, cut away torte from pan bottom. Return torte to cooling rack to cool completely.
12. Meanwhile, prepare Creamy Rum Filling.
13. Chop ½ cup (2 oz.) walnuts finely and set aside.
14. When torte is completely cooled, split into two layers. Place bottom half on a serving plate, cut side up. Spread with about one half of the filling. Cover with second layer, cut side down. Spread remaining filling over top of torte. Sprinkle with the finely chopped walnuts.

One 7-in torte

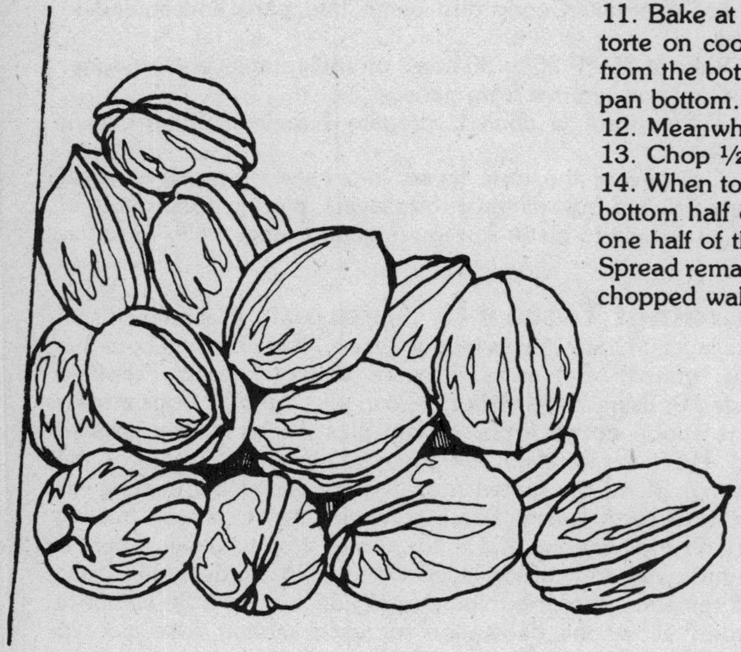

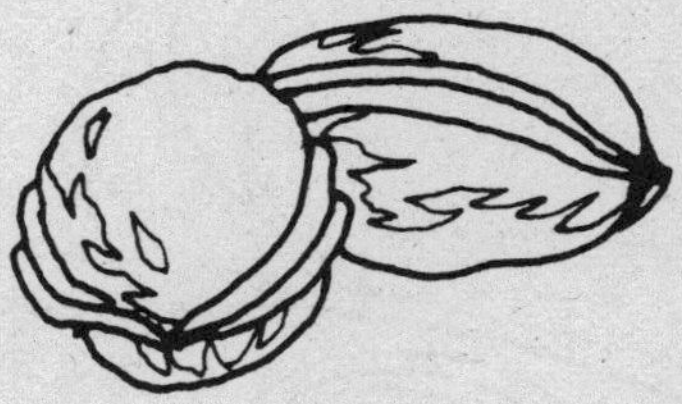

Dark Chocolate Frosting

- **4** **sq. (4 oz.) chocolate**
- **3** **tablespoons butter**
- **2¼** **cups sifted confectioners' sugar**
- **½** **cup top milk or cream**
- **1** **teaspoon vanilla extract**

1. Melt chocolate and butter together and stir until smooth.
2. Remove from heat and add confectioners' sugar, milk or cream, and vanilla extract.
3. Beat until of spreading consistency.

Enough to frost sides and tops of two 9-in. cake layers

Chocolate Torte

½ lb. almonds (about 3½ cups, grated)
1¼ cups cocoa
1 teaspoon cinnamon
1 cup unsalted butter
1½ teaspoons vanilla extract
⅔ cup sugar
8 egg yolks, unbeaten
8 egg whites
⅔ cup sugar
Chocolate-Mocha Butter-Cream Frosting (page 60)

1. Prepare three 9-in. round layer cake pans.
2. Blanch and grate ½ lb. almonds.
3. Sift together cocoa and cinnamon.
4. Mix almonds and cocoa mixture together. Turn onto a piece of waxed paper. Using a spatula, mark into four portions, and set aside.
5. Cream butter and vanilla extract together until butter is soft and fluffy.
6. Add ⅔ cup sugar gradually, creaming until fluffy after each addition.
7. Add egg yolks one at a time, beating until well blended and fluffy after each addition.
8. Beat an additional 2 min. after addition of last yolk. Set mixture aside.
9. Using clean beater, beat egg whites until frothy.
10. Add ⅔ cup sugar about 2 tablespoons at a time, beating well after each addition.
11. Beat the meringue until very stiff peaks are formed.
12. Gently spread beaten egg whites over egg-yolk mixture. Sprinkle one portion of the cocoa mixture over egg whites; gently fold with a few strokes until batter is only *partially* blended. Repeat with second and then third portions. Spoon remaining mixture over batter and gently fold until *just* blended. *Do not overmix!* Gently turn batter into pans and spread to edges.
13. Bake at 350°F 30 to 35 min., or until torte layers test done.
14. Cool; remove from pans as directed. When completely cooled, fill and frost torte layers with Chocolate-Mocha Butter-Cream Frosting.
15. Place in refrigerator until ready to serve.

12 to 16 servings

Note: **Butter-Cream Frosting** (page 60) or any variation except the Hazelnut may be used.

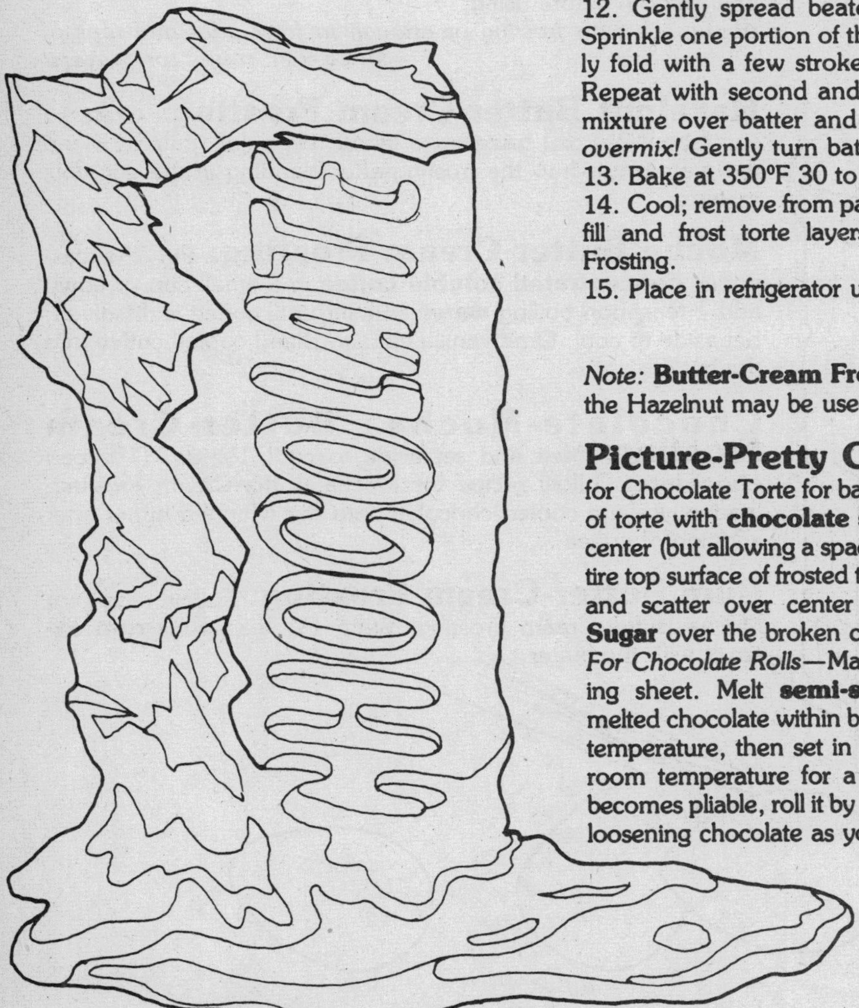

Picture-Pretty Chocolate Torte: Follow recipe for Chocolate Torte for baking and frosting torte layers. Cover sides of torte with **chocolate shot.** Set Chocolate Rolls radiating from center (but allowing a space at center) slightly over edge around entire top surface of frosted torte. Break several of the Rolls into pieces and scatter over center of torte. Sift **Vanilla Confectioners' Sugar** over the broken chocolate.

For Chocolate Rolls—Mark 3-in. squares on waxed paper on baking sheet. Melt **semi-sweet chocolate.** Spread 1 teaspoon melted chocolate within borders of each 3-in. square. Cool at room temperature, then set in refrigerator to harden. To roll, set out at room temperature for a few minutes. As chocolate softens and becomes pliable, roll it by slowly folding the waxed paper over itself, loosening chocolate as you roll it. Chill.

Butter-Cream Frosting

- **6 egg yolks**
- **¾ cup sugar**
- **½ teaspoon cornstarch**
- **¾ cup cream**
- **2 teaspoons vanilla extract**
- **1½ cups firm, unsalted butter**

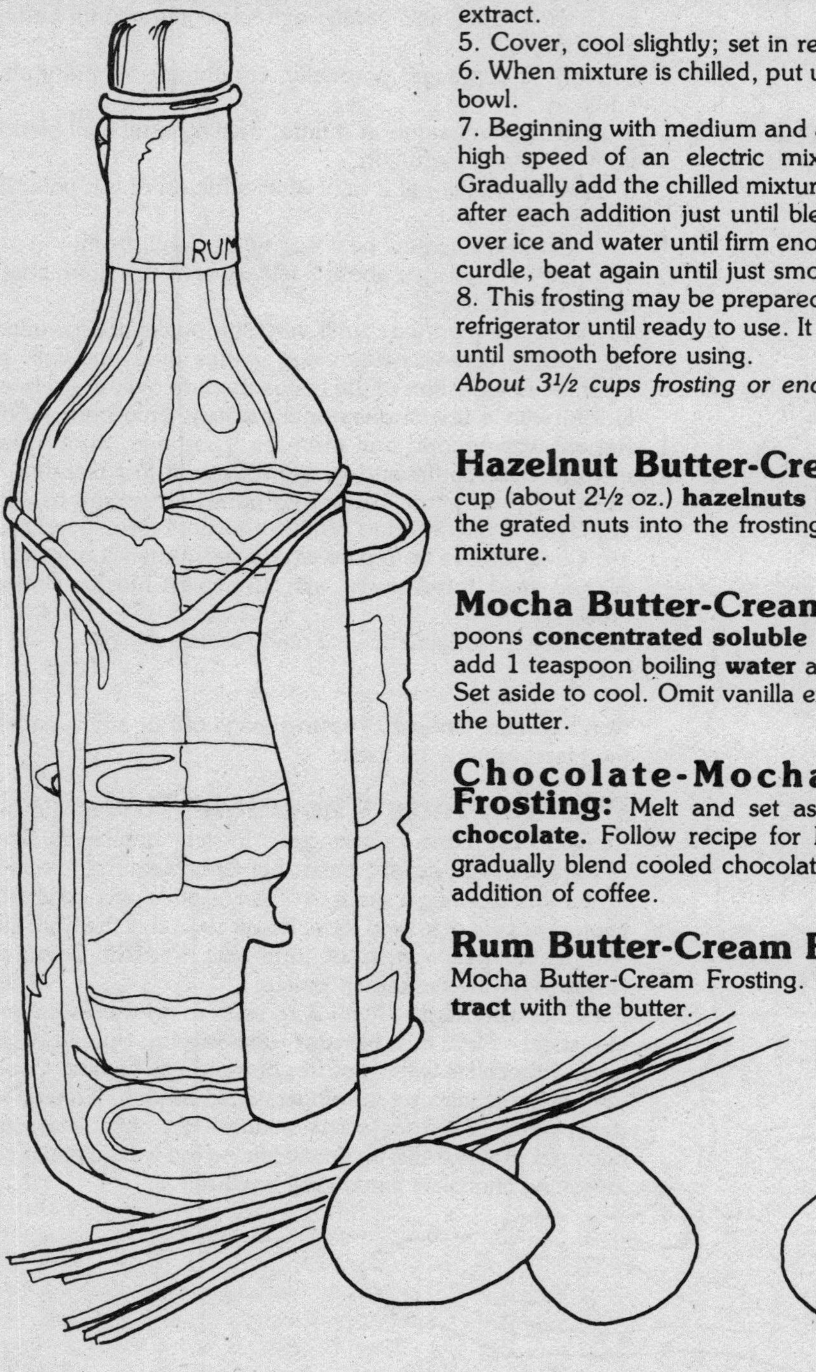

1. In top of a double boiler, beat egg yolks until thick and lemon-colored.
2. Add sugar and cornstarch gradually, beating constantly.
3. Add cream gradually and stir until well blended.
4. Set over simmering water and cook, stirring constantly, until thickened (about 17 min.). Remove from heat and stir in vanilla extract.
5. Cover, cool slightly; set in refrigerator to chill.
6. When mixture is chilled, put unsalted butter into a large mixer bowl.
7. Beginning with medium and as soon as possible increasing to high speed of an electric mixer, beat until butter is fluffy. Gradually add the chilled mixture to the creamed butter, beating after each addition just until blended. If necessary, set frosting over ice and water until firm enough to spread. If frosting should curdle, beat again until just smooth.
8. This frosting may be prepared, tightly covered, and placed in refrigerator until ready to use. It will keep several days. Beat just until smooth before using.

About 3½ cups frosting or enough to frost sides and tops of three 9-in. round torte layers.

Hazelnut Butter-Cream Frosting: Grate ½ cup (about 2½ oz.) **hazelnuts** (about 1½ cups, grated). Blend the grated nuts into the frosting after blending in the egg-yolk mixture.

Mocha Butter-Cream Frosting: Put 1¾ teaspoons **concentrated soluble coffee** in a small cup or bowl; add 1 teaspoon boiling **water** and stir until coffee is dissolved. Set aside to cool. Omit vanilla extract. Blend cooled coffee into the butter.

Chocolate-Mocha Butter-Cream Frosting: Melt and set aside to cool 1½ sq. (1½ oz.) **chocolate.** Follow recipe for Mocha Butter-Cream Frosting; gradually blend cooled chocolate into the whipped butter after addition of coffee.

Rum Butter-Cream Frosting: Follow recipe for Mocha Butter-Cream Frosting. Whip 1½ teaspoons **rum extract** with the butter.

Creamy Rum Filling

1½ cups cream
½ cup sugar
2½ tablespoons all-purpose flour
¼ teaspoon salt
3 egg yolks, slightly beaten
2 tablespoons rum
1 tablespoon butter

1. Set out cream.
2. Scald 1 cup of the cream; reserve remainder.
3. Meanwhile, sift together sugar, flour, and salt into a small saucepan.
4. Blend in the reserved cream; add gradually and stir in the scalded cream. Bring rapidly to boiling over direct heat, stirring gently and constantly; cook 3 min. Remove from heat.
5. Wash the double-boiler top to remove scum; pour cream mixture into it and place over simmering water. Cover and cook about 5 to 7 min., stirring three or four times.
6. Vigorously stir about 3 tablespoons of the hot filling into egg yolks.
7. Immediately blend into filling mixture in the double boiler. Cook over simmering water 3 to 5 min., stirring slowly and constantly to keep mixture cooking evenly.
8. Remove from heat and blend in rum and butter.
9. Cover, cool slightly and chill in refrigerator.

About 1⅔ cups filling

Creamy Vanilla Filling: Substitute 2 teaspoons **vanilla extract** and ¼ teaspoon **almond extract** for rum.

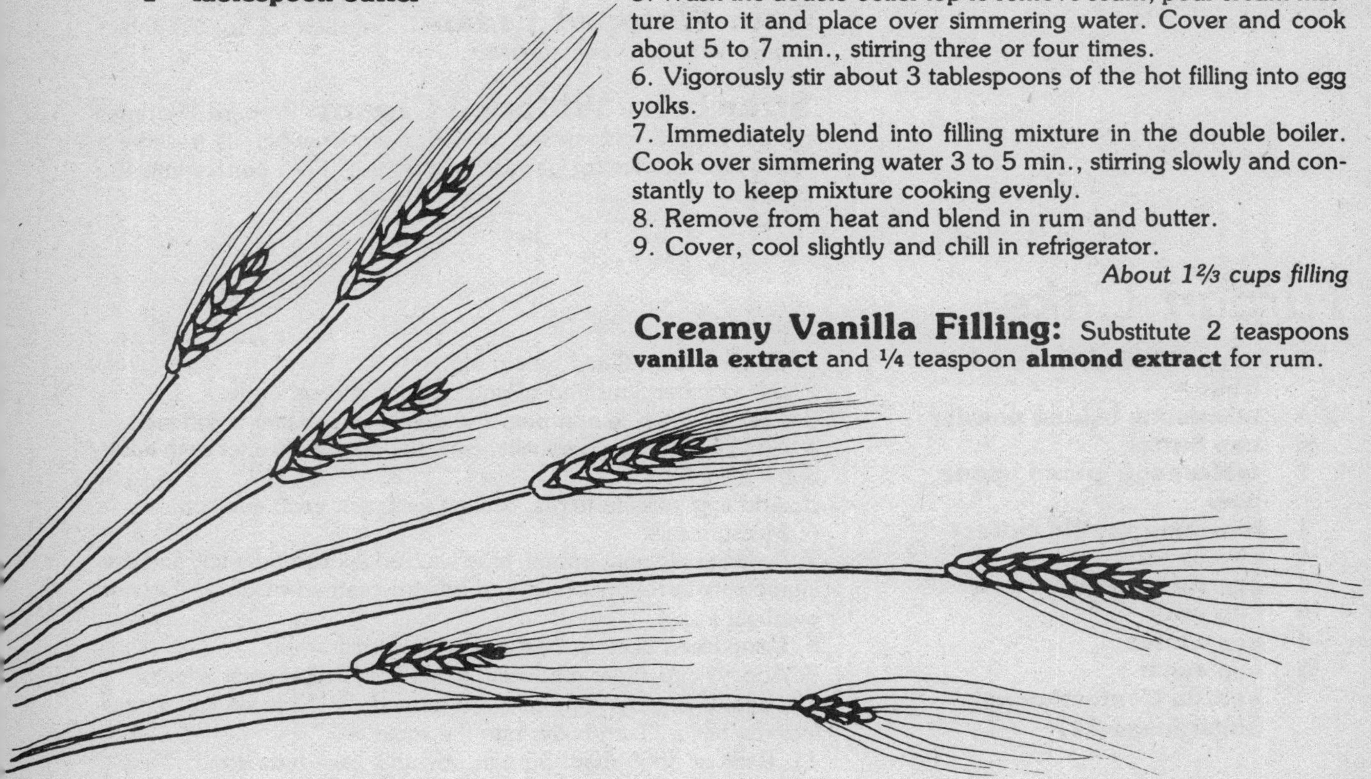

Vanilla Confectioners' Sugar

Confectioners' sugar
1 vanilla bean, about 9 in. long

1. Set out a 1- to 2-qt. container having a tight-fitting cover. Fill with sugar.
2. Remove vanilla bean from air-tight tube, wipe with a clean, damp cloth and dry.
3. Cut vanilla bean into quarters lengthwise; cut quarters crosswise into thirds. Poke pieces of vanilla bean down into the sugar at irregular intervals. Cover container tightly and store on pantry shelf.
4. Use on cookies, cakes, tortes, rolled pancakes or wherever a sprinkling of confectioners' sugar is desired.

Note: The longer sugar stands, the richer will be the vanilla flavor. If tightly covered, sugar may be stored for several months. When necessary, add more sugar to jar. Replace vanilla bean when aroma is gone.

Sweetened Whipped Cream

1 cup chilled whipping cream
¼ cup sifted confectioners' sugar
1 teaspoon vanilla extract

1. Place a rotary beater and a 1-qt. bowl in refrigerator to chill.
2. Using chilled bowl and beater, beat until cream stands in peaks when beater is slowly lifted upright.
3. Beat sugar and vanilla extract into whipped cream with final few strokes until blended.
4. Set in refrigerator if not used immediately.

About 2 cups whipped cream

Rum Whipped Cream: Substitute 1 to 1½ tablespoons **rum** for vanilla extract.

Strawberry Whipped Cream: Prepare 1½ times recipe. Slice 2 pints rinsed, hulled, fresh strawberries (reserve a few whole berries for garnish, if desired). Fold berries into the cream.

Turban Cake

2 cups sifted all-purpose flour
2¼ teaspoons baking powder
½ cup butter
1 tablespoon grated lemon peel
1 teaspoon vanilla extract
½ cup sugar
4 egg yolks, well beaten
¾ cup milk
4 egg whites
½ cup sugar
Vanilla Confectioners' Sugar (page 61)

1. Butter a 2-qt. fluted tube mold.
2. Sift together flour and baking powder and set aside.
3. Cream butter, lemon peel and vanilla until butter is softened.
4. Add ½ cup sugar gradually, creaming until fluffy after each addition.
5. Add egg yolks in thirds, beating well after each addition.
6. Measure milk.
7. Beating only until smooth after each addition, alternately add dry ingredients in fourths, milk in thirds to creamed mixture. (Do not overbeat.)
8. Using clean beaters, beat egg whites until frothy.
9. Add ½ cup sugar gradually, beating well after each addition.
10. Beat until very stiff peaks are formed. Fold beaten egg whites into the batter. Turn batter into the mold.
11. Bake at 350° about 55 min., or until cake tests done.
12. Invert pan on tube end and let cake hang in pan 1 hr. If cake is higher than tube, invert between two cooling racks so top of cake does not touch any surface.
13. Remove from pan by running a paring knife or small spatula carefully around tube and around edge of cake. Serve slightly warm, if desired. Sprinkle cake generously with Vanilla Confectioners' Sugar.

8 to 10 servings

Poppy Seed Cake: Set out ½ cup (about 1½ oz.) freshly ground **poppy seeds.** Just before first addition of dry ingredients, blend in the poppy seeds.

Chocolate-Glazed Cake: Partially melt over hot (not simmering) water, being careful not to overheat, ¼ lb. **semisweet candymaking chocolate** and ¼ lb. **butter.** Remove from the hot water and stir until chocolate is completely melted. Quickly spread over the cake while mixture is still warm. Let chocolate cool completely before serving.

Cheese Cake

1 cup sifted all-purpose flour
2 tablespoons sugar
¼ teaspoon salt
¼ cup softened butter
1 egg, slightly beaten
2¼ cups (about 12 oz.) blanched almonds; about 5⅓ cups grated)
1 16 oz. can pitted red tart cherries
1 lb. (2 cups) dry cottage cheese
1 cup butter
2 teaspoons grated lemon peel
1 cup sugar
7 egg yolks
7 egg whites
¾ cup sugar

1. Set out a 9-in. spring-form pan.
2. *For Crust*-Sift together into a bowl flour, sugar, and salt.
3. Make a well in center of flour, and in well work butter and egg to a creamy mixture.
4. Quickly and thoroughly mix with the flour. Shape dough into ball and wrap in waxed paper. Set in refrigerator to chill about 2 hrs.
5. Put dough out on lightly floured surface and flatten. Roll from center to edge into a round about ¼ in. thick. With a knife or spatula, loosen pastry from surface whenever sticking occurs; lift pastry slightly and sprinkle flour under it.
6. With spatula, loosen pastry from board and fold it in half, then in quarters. Gently lay it in pan and unfold pastry without stretching, fitting it to bottom of pan only.
7. Bake at 450°F 10 min.
8. Set aside on cooling rack to cool.
9. *For Filling*-Grate and set aside almonds.
10. Set aside to drain thoroughly, contents of cherries.
11. Force cottage cheese through a sieve or food mill into a bowl and set aside.
12. Cream together butter and lemon peel until softened.
13. Add 1 cup sugar gradually, creaming until fluffy after each addition.
14. Beat egg yolks until thick and lemon-colored.
15. Add the beaten egg yolks in thirds to the creamed mixture, beating thoroughly after each addition. Beat in the cheese and the grated almonds. Set aside.
16. Lightly butter the sides of the spring-form pan.
17. Using clean beater, beat egg whites until frothy.
18. Add ¾ cup sugar gradually, beating well after each addition.
19. Continue beating until very stiff peaks are formed. Gently fold into the cheese mixture.
20. Arrange the well-drained cherries in an even layer over the cooled crust. Gently turn the cheese mixture into the pan; spread evenly.
21. Bake at 300°F about 1 hr. and 30 min. Let stand in oven 1 hr. longer. Remove to cooling rack to cool completely (about 4 hrs.). Set in refrigerator to chill.
22. Carefully run a spatula around inside of pan from top to bottom to loosen cake. Remove sides of pan. If desired sprinkle edges of Cheese Cake with sifted **confectioners' sugar.**

About 16 servings

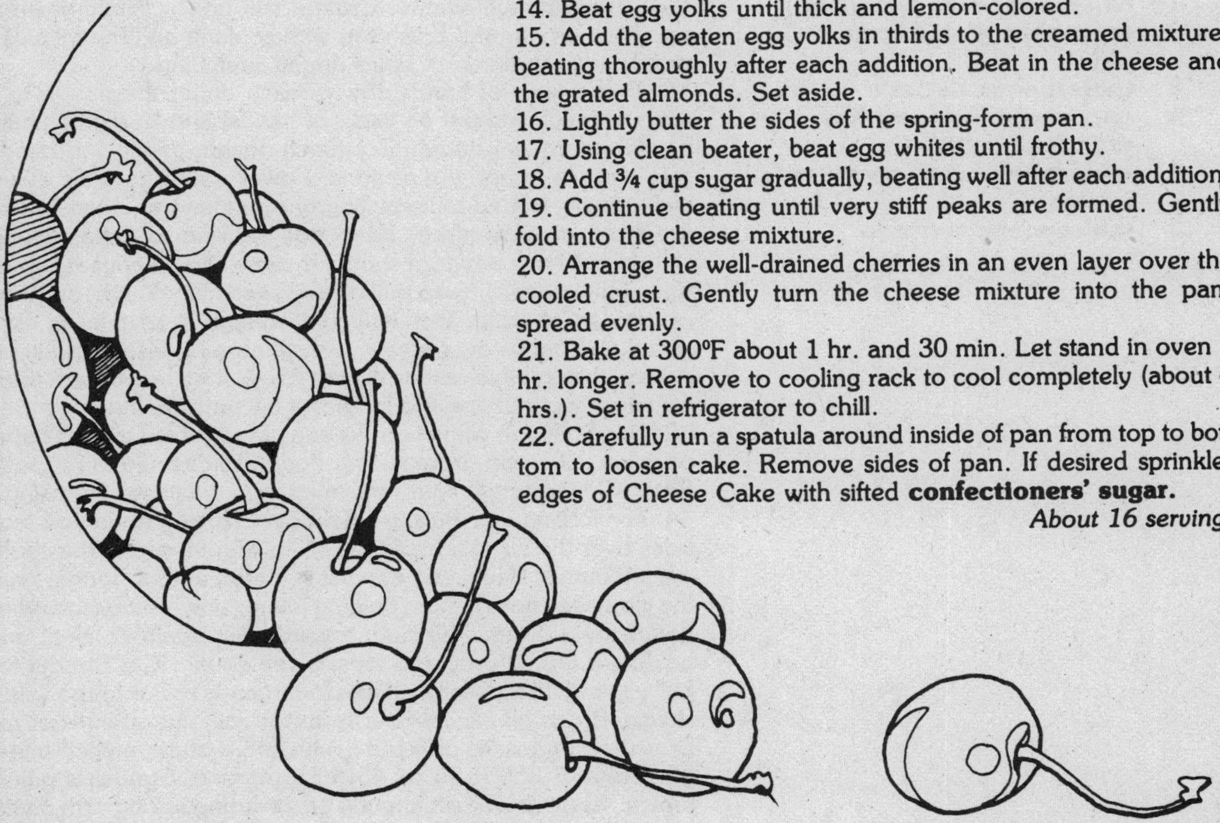

Apple Strudel

- **3 cups sifted all-purpose flour**
- **½ teaspoon salt**
- **1 egg, beaten**
- **1 tablespoon cooking oil**
- **1 cup lukewarm (80°F to 85°F) water**
- **Cooking oil (not olive oil)**
- **1 cup butter**
- **½ cup all-purpose flour**
- **Confectioners' sugar or Vanilla Confectioners' Sugar (page 61)**
- **Sweetened Whipped Cream (page 62)**
- **4 medium-size (about 1½ lbs.) cooking apples**
- **2 tablespoons vanilla extract**
- **2 tablespoons brown sugar**
- **2 tablespoons sugar**
- **1½ teaspoons cinnamon**
- **½ teaspoon allspice**
- **2 tablespoons brown sugar**
- **1 cup (about 4 oz.) walnuts**
- **2 teaspoons grated lemon peel**
- **2 tablespoons butter**
- **¾ cup (about 2 slices) fine dry bread crumbs**
- **2 tablespoons dark seedless raisins**
- **3 tablespoons currants**

1. Generously butter 2 baking sheets.
2. *For Strudel Dough*-Put 3 cups sifted all-purpose flour and salt into a large bowl and make a well in center.
3. Add egg and 1 tablespoon cooking oil and mix well.
4. Stirring constantly to keep mixture a smooth paste, add water gradually.
5. Mix until a soft dough is formed (the dough will be sticky). Turn dough out onto a lightly floured pastry board. Hold dough high above board and hit it hard against the board about 100 to 125 times, or until the dough is smooth and elastic and leaves the board easily. (After 15 or 20 times it will no longer stick.)
6. Knead slightly and pat into a round. Lightly brush top of dough with cooking oil.
7. Cover dough with an inverted bowl and allow it to rest 30 min.
8. Meanwhile, see filling recipe; prepare apples, bread crumbs, nuts and sugar mixture.
9. Melt butter and set aside to cool.
10. Cover a table (about 48x30 in.) with a clean cloth, allowing cloth to hang down, and sprinkle with flour (most in center of cloth).
11. Place dough on center of cloth and roll into a 12-in. square. If necessary, sprinkle more flour under dough so it does not stick. Keep dough square. Using a soft brush, lightly brush off any flour on top and brush top with cooking oil (The oil aids in preventing formation of holes during stretching.)
12. With palms of hands down, reach under the dough to its center (dough will rest on backs of hands) and lift slightly, being careful not to tear dough. To stretch dough, gently and steadily pull arms in opposite directions. Lower dough to table as you walk slowly around table pulling one side and another, but not too much in one place. Keep dough close to table. (Dough should not have any torn spots. If some should appear, do not try to patch them.) Keep pulling and stretching dough, draping it over edge of table. Continue until dough is as thin as tissue paper and hangs over edges of table on all sides. With kitchen shears, trim off thick outer edges. Allow stretched dough to dry 10 min. Avoid drying too long as it becomes brittle.
13. Drizzle dough with about ¼ cup of the cooled melted butter. Sprinkle the bread drumbs over dough as directed in recipe for filling. Cover dough with remaining ingredients for the filling.
14. *For Rolling and Baking*—Fold overhanging dough on three sides over the filling. Drizzle the filling with ½ cup of the cooled melted butter. Beginning at narrow folded end of dough, grasp the cloth with both hands, holding it taut; slowly lift cloth and roll dough over filling. Pull cloth toward you; again lift cloth and, holding it taut, slowly and loosely roll dough. Cut Strudel into halves, and lifting each half on cloth, gently roll onto the baking sheets. Brush off excess flour from the roll; cut off ends of roll. Brush top and sides of Strudel with some of the melted butter.
15. Bake at 350ºF 35 to 45 min., or until Strudel is golden brown. Baste and brush about 4 times during baking with melted butter. When Strudel makes a crackly sound on touching it is done. (Strudel should not be smooth.)

16. Remove to cooling rack; cool slightly. Sift Confectioners' sugar or Vanilla Confectioners' Sugar over top of strudel.
17. Remove to a cutting board. Cut Strudel into 2-in. slices and serve warm with **Sweetened Whipped Cream.**

12 slices

18. *For Filling*—Wash, quarter, core and pare apples.
19. Cut apples into slices about 1/8 in. thick and put into a bowl with vanilla extract and 2 tablespoons brown sugar.
20. Toss lightly to coat slices evenly. Set aside for at least 30 min., tossing occasionally.
21. Mix together sugar, cinnamon, and allspice.
22. Blend in 2 tablespoons brown sugar.
23. Chop walnuts finely and set aside.
24. Grate lemon peel and set aside.
25. Heat a skillet over medium heat. Add butter and melt quickly.
26. Toss bread crumbs in the butter until browned and thoroughly coated.
27. Sprinkle the bread crumbs evenly over one-half the stretched and slightly dry bread.
28. Drain the apples and cover crumbs evenly with the slices. Sprinkle lemon peel over apples. Toss evenly over apples the nuts and raisins and currants.
29. Sprinkle sugar mixture over nuts and fruit. Drizzle with melted butter.

Marble Cake

3½ cups sifted cake flour
1 tablespoon baking powder
½ teaspoon salt
1 cup butter
1 teaspoon almond extract
1½ cups sugar
4 eggs, well beaten
1 cup milk
¼ cup sugar
¼ cup cocoa
¼ 3 tablespoons rum
Creamy Rum Filling (page 61)
Dark Chocolate Frosting (page 58)

1. Prepare two 9-in. round layer cake pans.
2. Sift together flour, baking powder, and salt, and set aside.
3. Cream together butter and almond extract until softened.
4. Add 1½ cups sugar gradually, creaming until fluffy after each addition.
5. Add eggs in thirds, beating thoroughly after each addition.
6. Measure milk.
7. Beating only until smooth after each addition, alternately add dry ingredients in fourths, milk in thirds, to creamed mixture. Finally beat only until smooth (do not overbeat). Divide the batter into two equal portions and turn one portion into the two prepared cake pans.
8. Blend ¼ cup sugar, cocoa, and rum together thoroughly.
9. Gently blend cocoa mixture into remaining batter. Turn one-half of the chocolate batter over the yellow batter in each pan. With a spatula, gently lift yellow batter through chocolate batter to produce marbled effect, but do not overblend.
10. Bake at 350°F 35 to 40 min., or until cake tests done. Cool and remove from pans as directed.
11. When cake is cooled, prepare Creamy Rum Filling and Dark Chocolate Frosting.
12. Fill and frost as directed.

One 9-inch round layer cake

Emperor's Dessert

2 tablespoons butter
1 cup sifted all-purpose flour
¼ cup sugar
¼ teaspoon salt
3 eggs
1 cup milk
¾ cup butter
½ cup golden raisins
½ teaspoon cinnamon
1 cup sugar

1. *For Pancakes*—Lightly butter a 6-in skillet.
2. Melt 2 tablespoons butter and set aside.
3. Sift together flour, sugar, and salt into a bowl and set aside.
4. Beat eggs until thick and piled softly.
5. Beat milk in the melted butter.
6. Combine egg mixture with dry ingredients and beat with rotary beater until smooth.
7. Heat skillet moderately hot. Pour in just enough batter to cover bottom. Immediately tilt skillet back and forth to spread batter thinly and evenly.
8. Cook over medium heat until light brown on bottom and firm to touch on top. Loosen edge with spatula. Turn and brown second side. It should be unnecessary to grease skillet for each pancake.
9. As each pancake is cooked, transfer to a hot platter. When all are cooked, set platter in warm oven to keep pancakes warm.
10. *For Sauce*—Melt ¾ cup butter over low heat in a suacepan.
11. Stir in raisins and cinnamon.
12. Add ¾ to 1 cup sugar and mix very lightly.
13. Do not stir sugar too much. It should not be dissolved in the butter.
14. *To Complete Dessert*—Tear Pancakes with two forks into 1-in. irregular pieces. Mix into the sauce.

Witches' Snow

½ cup cold water
1 env. unflavored gelatin
2 cups (16 oz. can) thick, sweetened applesauce
¾ cup sugar
½ cup apricot preserves
2 tablespoons rum
1 teaspoon lemon juice
2 egg whites

A 2-qt. mold will be needed.

1. Pour water into a small cup or custard cup.
2. Sprinkle unflavored gelatin evenly over cold water.
3. Let stand until softened. Meanwhile mix applesauce, sugar, preserves, rum and lemon juice in a large bowl.
4. Dissolve gelatin completely by placing over very hot water. Stir gelatin into applesauce mixture. Stir until sugar is completely dissolved.
5. Chill in refrigerator or in a pan of ice and water until mixture begins to gel (gets slightly thicker). (If mixture is placed over ice and water, stir frequently; if placed in refrigerator, stir occasionally.)
6. Meanwhile, lightly oil the mold with salad or cooking oil (not olive oil). Set aside to drain.
7. When mixture is of desired consistency, add egg whites.
8. Beat with electric mixer or rotary beater until mixture is very thick and piles softly (about 14 min.). Turn into the mold.
9. Chill in refrigerator until firm (about 4½ hrs.).
10. When ready to serve, unmold onto chilled serving plate. Garnish base of mold with any **fresh fruit** in season.

8 to 10 servings

Apple Pancakes

3 small firm cooking apples(about 2½ cups, sliced)
¼ cup butter
2 tablespoons sugar
1 teaspoon cinnamon
½ cup sifted all-purpose flour
1 tablespoon sugar
¼ teaspoon salt
4 eggs
⅓ cup milk
6 tablespoons butter
Melted butter
Confectioners' sugar

1. Set out a 10-in. skillet.
2. Wash, quarter, core and pare apples.
3. Thinly slice the apples. Heat ¼ cup butter in the skillet over low heat.
4. Add apple slices, cover and cook over medium heat until apples are almost tender, moving and turning slices with a spoon several times during cooking. When apple slices are almost tender, sprinkle over them and gently blend in a mixture of 2 tablespoons sugar and cinnamon.
5. Continue cooking, uncovered, until apples are *just* tender. Turn apple mixture into a bowl and set aside to keep warm.
6. Sift flour, 1 tablespoon sugar, and salt together into a bowl and set aside.
7. Beat eggs until thick and piled softly.
8. Beat in milk.
9. Combine egg mixture with dry ingredients and beat with rotary beater until smooth. Set aside.
10. Set out 6 tablespoons butter.
11. Add 3 tablespoons of the butter to the skillet and heat until moderately hot.
12. Spoon in enough batter to cover bottom of skillet. Spoon about one-half of apple mixture evenly over batter. Spoon in more batter, to just cover apples. Cook pancakes over medium heat until golden brown on bottom. Loosen edges with spatula. Carefully turn and brown other side.
13. When pancake is cooked, remove skillet from heat and brush pancake generously with melted butter.
14. Roll up pancake and transfer to a warm platter.
15. Sift Confectioners' sugar over top.
16. Keep pancake hot. Repeat procedure.

2 Apple Pancakes

Rice and Apple Pudding

3 cups milk
½ cup rice
¼ teaspoon salt
½ cup butter
1 tablespoon grated lemon peel
⅓ cup sugar
4 egg yolks, well beaten
¼ cup dark seedless raisins
3 medium-size apples
4 egg whites
2 tablespoons sugar
Confectioners' sugar

A 2-qt. baking dish will be needed.

1. Put milk, rice, and salt into the top of a double boiler. (The Rice Industry no longer considers it necessary to wash rice before cooking.)
2. Cover and cook over simmering water 1¾ to 2 hrs., or until rice is entirely soft when a kernel is pressed between fingers and the mixture is quite thick.
3. Butter the baking dish.
4. Just before rice is thick, cream butter and lemon peel together until butter is softened.
5. Add sugar gradually, creaming until fluffy after each addition.
6. Blend in egg yolks in thirds, beating thoroughly after each addition.
7. Blend in the rice and raisins.
8. Wash, quarter, core and pare apples.
9. Cut into very thin slices. Set aside.
10. Beat egg whites until stiff, not dry, peaks are formed.
11. Gently fold beaten egg whites into the rice mixture. Turn one-half of the mixture into the greased baking dish. Arrange apples on top of rice mixture. Sprinkle with **1 to 2 tablespoons sugar (depending upon tartness of apples).**
12. Turn remaining rice mixture into baking dish.
13. Bake at 325°F 60 to 65 min., or until lightly browned. Sprinkle with **Confectioners' sugar.** Serve warm.

6 to 8 servings

Farina Pudding

2 cups milk
2 tablespoons butter
1½ teaspoons grated lemon peel
¼ teaspoon salt
⅓ cup farina
4 egg yolks
4 egg whites
¼ cup sugar

1. Heat the water for hot water bath. Butter a 2-qt. casserole.
2. Scald milk in top of double boiler.
3. Add and stir in butter, lemon peel and salt.
4. Add farina gradually, stirring constantly.
5. Cook over simmering water 20 min. or until thick, stirring constantly. Remove from simmering water and turn mixture into a medium-size bowl. Cool to lukewarm, stirring occasionally.
6. Beat egg yolks until thick and lemon-colored.
7. Blend into cooled mixture and set aside.
8. Beat egg whites until frothy.
9. Add sugar gradually, beating well after each addition.
10. Continue to beat until very stiff peaks are formed. Spread beaten egg whites over farina mixture and gently fold together. Turn mixture into casserole.
11. Bake in the hot water bath at 325°F 1 hr. 35 min., or until surface is lightly browned and a silver knife inserted halfway between center and edge of casserole comes out clean. Serve at once.

6 to 8 servings

—Farina Pudding with Apricots: Before turning mixture into casserole, arrange over bottom of casserole ¼ lb. dried apricots which have been cooked until just tender, following package directions; drain if necessary.

Black Forest Torte

- **1½ cups toasted filberts, grated***
- **¼ cup flour**
- **½ cup butter or margarine**
- **1 cup sugar**
- **6 egg yolks**
- **4 oz. (4 sq.) semisweet chocolate, melted and cooled**
- **6 tablespoons kirsch**
- **6 egg whites**
- **Cherry Filling, below**
- **3 cups chilled heavy cream**
- **⅓ cup confectioners' sugar**
- **Chocolate curls**

1. Grease and lightly flour an 8-inch springform pan; set aside.
2. Blend grated filberts and flour; set aside.
3. Cream butter until softened. Beat in sugar gradually until mixture is light and fluffy. Add egg yolks, one at a time, beating thoroughly after each addition.
4. Blend in the chocolate and 2 tablespoons of the kirsch. Stir in nut-flour mixture until blended.
5. Beat egg whites until stiff, not dry, peaks are formed. Fold into batter and turn into the pan.
6. Bake at 375°F about 1 hour, or until torte tests done. (Torte should be about 1½ inches high and top may have a slight crack.)
7. Cool 10 minutes in pan on a wire rack; remove from pan and cool.
8. Using a long sharp knife, carefully cut torte into 3 layers. Place top layer inverted on a cake plate; spread with Cherry Filling.
9. Whip cream (1½ cups at a time) until soft peaks are formed, gradually adding half of the confectioners' sugar and 2 tablespoons of the kirsch to each portion.
10. Generously spread some of the whipped cream over the Cherry Filling. Cover with second layer and remaining Cherry Filling. Spread generously with more whipped cream and top with third torte layer. Frost entire torte with remaining whipped cream.
11. Decorate torte with reserved cherries and chocolate curls.

One 8-inch torte

*To grate nuts, use a rotary-type grater with hand-operated crank.

Cherry Filling: Drain 1 jar (16 ounces) *red maraschino cherries*, reserving ½ cup syrup. Set aside 13 cherries for decoration; slice remaining cherries. Set aside. Combine reserved syrup and 4 *tablespoons kirsch*. In a saucepan, gradually blend syrup mixture into 1½ *tablespoons cornstarch*. Mix in 1 *tablespoon lemon juice*. Stir over medium heat until mixture boils ½ minute. Mix in sliced cherries and cool.

1⅓ cups filling

Raisin Cake

- **5¼ oz. butter or margarine at room temperature**
- **3 eggs**
- **2 teaspoons lemon peel, grated**
- **2 tablespoons lemon juice or rum**
- **½-¾ cup raisins**
- **2 cups all-purpose flour**
- **2 teaspoons baking powder**
- **½ cup milk**
- **bread crumbs**
- **confectioners' sugar**

1. Beat butter and sugar until foamy. Add eggs one at a time, beating vigorously after each.
2. Then add lemon peel, lemon juice, raisins mixed with 2 tablespoons flour, remainder of flour mixed with baking powder and milk.
3. Butter baking dish and sprinkle with bread crumbs. Pour in batter and bake in 350°F oven for 50-60 minutes. Sprinkle with confectioners' sugar after cooling.

Hazelnut Torte with Strawberry Whipped Cream

Graham cracker crumbs (about 3 tablespoons)
2 cups sugar
½ teaspoon ground allspice
1 teaspoon grated lemon peel
4 cups (about 1b.) filberts or hazelnuts, grated in rotary-type grater
6 egg yolks (½ cup)
6 egg whites (¾ cup)
¼ teaspoon salt
1 tablespoon light corn syrup
1 teaspoon water
1 egg white, slightly beaten
Strawberry Whipped Cream, page 62

1. Thoroughly grease a 6½-cup ring mold and coat evenly with graham cracker crumbs; set aside.
2. Blend sugar, allspice, and lemon peel in a large bowl; mix in filberts until completely blended.
3. Beat egg yolks until thick and lemon colored. Using a fork, blend into nut mixture.
4. Using a clean bowl and beater, beat the egg whites with the salt until stiff, not dry, peaks are formed. Blend into nut mixture. Turn into prepared mold; spread evenly using the back of a spoon.
5. Bake at 350°F 45 to 55 minutes.
6. Remove torte from oven (leave oven on); cool 10 to 15 minutes on a wire rack. Loosen torte from mold and turn out onto an ungreased baking sheet.
7. Blend corn syrup and water; brush over top of torte. Brush entire torte with egg white. Return torte to oven for 5 minutes.
8. Transfer to cake plate. Serve warm or at room temperature with Strawberry Whipped Cream.

One 9-inch Torte

Nutcake

5¼ oz. almonds
3 eggs
¾ cup sugar
½ teaspoon baking powder

Filling:
1 package pineapple mousse
½ cup heavy cream

Garnish:
½ can pineapples
½ cup heavy cream
1 teaspoon vanilla sugar
green citron pieces

1. Grind almonds. Beat eggs and sugar until foamy. Add almonds and baking powder.
2. Butter a baking dish well and sprinkle with bread crumbs. Pour in batter. Bake cake in 350°F oven about 40 minutes.
3. Remove cake from baking dish when cooled and sprinkle with pineapple juice.
4. Prepare pineapple mousse according to package directions and place on top of cake. Garnish with pineapple slices, citron pieces and whipped cream.

14 servings

Cookies

In addition to being the home of the Christmas tree, Germany is the home of many of the cookies which are associated by tradition with the cheerful festivities of our own Christmas seasons. Springerle and Pfeffernusse represent this group. Germany and Vienna have many other wonderful cookies, and one that truly defies description is the delicate chocolate-frosted Florentine.

Hazelnut Balls

1½ cups (about 6 oz.) hazelnuts
2 egg whites
1 cup sugar

1. Lightly grease cookie sheets.
2. Grate hazelnuts and set aside.
3. Beat egg whites until frothy.
4. Add about 2 tablespoons sugar at a time, beating well after each addition. Continue beating the meringue until stiff peaks are formed.
5. Fold the hazelnuts into the meringue mixture. Shape dough into balls about ½ in. in diameter. Place on the cookie sheets.
6. Bake at 300°F 25 min.
7. With a spatula, carefully remove cookies from cookie sheets to cooling racks.

About 4 doz. cookies

Flaky Layers

2 small (about ½ lb.) potatoes
2 cups sifted all-purpose flour
¼ cup sifted confectioners' sugar
1 cup firm butter
1 teaspoon vanilla extract
Currant jelly (or another jelly)

1. Wash and scrub potatoes with a vegetable brush.
2. Cook about 30 min., or until tender when pierced with a fork. Drain. Dry potatoes by shaking pan over low heat. Set potatoes aside to cool completely.
3. Meanwhile, sift together flour and sugar into a bowl. Cover tightly and set in refrigerator to chill.
4. Peel cold potatoes and force through a sieve or food mill. Measure 1 cup of the sieved potato. Remove flour mixture from refrigerator and add potato. Using a fork, gently mix together. Cut in butter with pastry blender or two knives until pieces are size of small peas.
5. Sprinkle vanilla extract gradually over mixture, a few drops at a time.
6. Mix lightly with a fork after each addition. Dough should be crumbly. Shape into a ball wrap in waxed paper, and chill in refrigerator several hours.
7. Set out two cookie sheets.
8. Remove dough from refrigerator and divide into two balls. Return one ball to refrigerator. Put other ball on a lightly floured surface. Roll dough ¼ in. thick in diameter. Using a cookie cutter ¾ in. in diameter, cut out centers from one-half of the cookie rounds so that a ring shape is formed. Place rounds, rings, and centers on one of the cookie sheets.
9. Bake at 400°F 10 to 15 min.
10. With spatula, remove cookies to cooling racks. Cool completely.
11. Repeat above procedure for remainder of dough, using second cookie sheet.
12. When all the cookies are cooled, set out Currant jelly (or another jelly).
13. Spread jelly thinly on cookie rounds. Top with rings. Fill centers of rings with a small amount of jelly. Top with centers.

About 2 doz. cookies

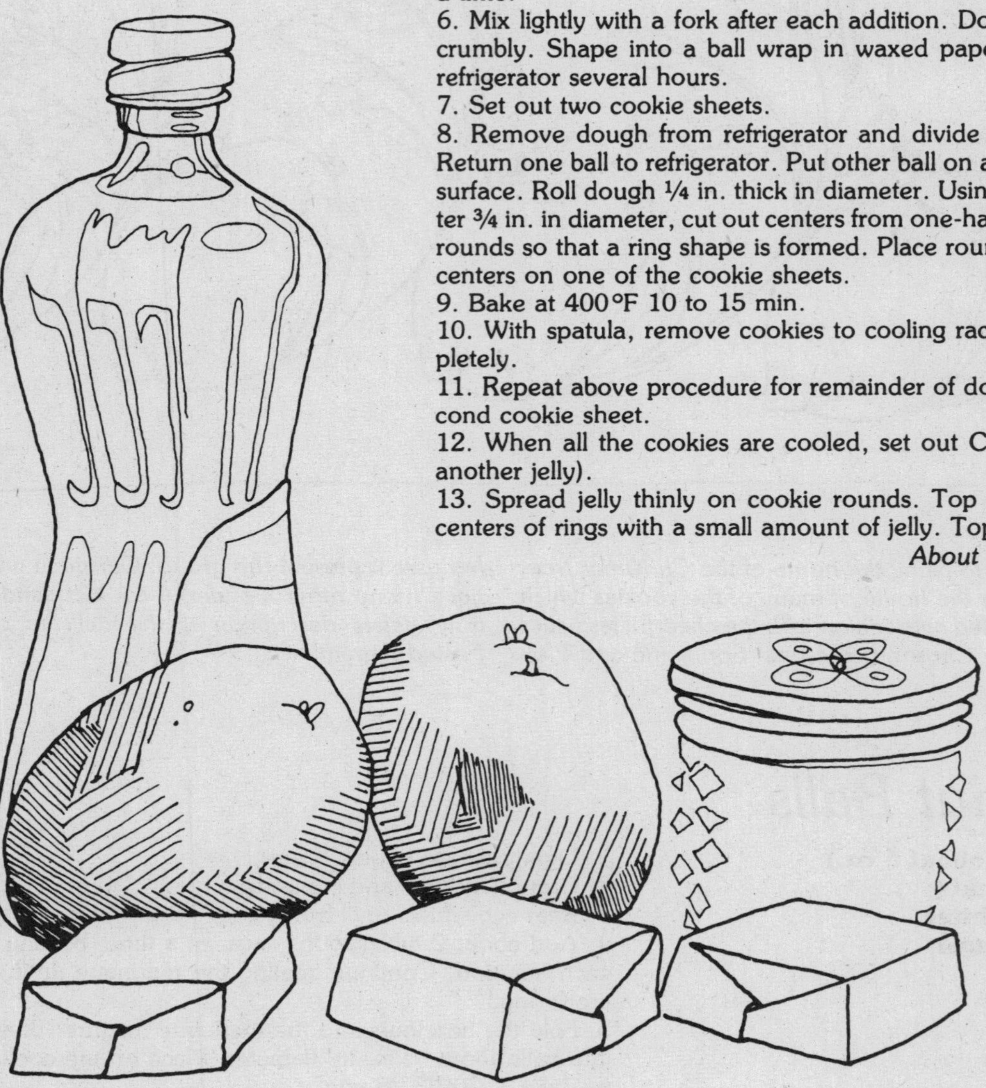

Florentines I

- **4 oz. (about ¾ cup) almonds (about 1 cup, slivered)**
- **3 oz. candied orange peel (about ½ cup, chopped)**
- **¾ cup sifted cake flour**
- **¼ teaspoon salt**
- **⅓ cup firmly packed light brown sugar**
- **¼ cup butter**
- **2 tablespoons honey**
- **2 tablespoons light corn syrup**
- **1 tablespoon heavy cream**
- **6 sq. (6 oz.) semi-sweet candymaking chocolate**
- **6 tablespoons butter**

1. Butter cookie sheets. Sprinkle lightly with flour; shake off excess flour.
2. Blanch, sliver and set almonds aside.
3. Chop orange peel finely and set aside.
4. Sift together flour and salt and set aside.
5. Rub sugar through coarse sieve.
6. Cream ¼ cup butter until softened.
7. Add sugar gradually, creaming until light and fluffy after each addition. Add gradually, beating in honey, corn syrup and heavy cream.
8. Add the almonds and chopped candied peel and mix well. Gradually add dry ingredients, blending thoroughly. Drop dough by level tablespoons onto the cookie sheet about 3 in. apart and spread into 2-in. rounds.
9. Bake at 350°F 7 min., or until cookies are delicately browned. The cookies will be about 3 in. in diameter with a slightly lacy appearance.
10. Remove cookie sheets to cooling racks and let cool 2 to 3 min. (Cookies must be warm to be removed.) Carefully remove cookies with a spatula (they may stick slightly to pan); place flat side up on cooling racks to cool.
11. When cookies are cooled, heat chocolate and 6 tablespoons butter until chocolate is partially melted, being careful not to overheat.
12. Remove from the hot water and stir until chocolate is completely melted. Cool mixture to lukewarm.
13. Carefully spread about 1½ teaspoons of chocolate mixture over flat side of each cookie spreading to edges. Let stand until chocolate is almost set. Using a fork, carefully draw wavy lines through the chocolate.

About 26 cookies

Florentines II

Decrease almonds to 1½ oz. (¼ cup) and grate (about ¾ cup grated). Omit candied orange peel. Decrease flour to ¼ cup plus 2 tablespoons. Cream 2 tablespoons grated **lemon peel** and ½ teaspoon **almond extract** with butter. Blend in the almonds before addition of dry ingredients. Drop by heaping teaspoons about 3 in. apart onto cookie sheets. Bake at 350°F 10 min., or until cookies are golden brown. The cookies should be very thin, about 4 in. in diameter, and have a lacy appearance. Decrease chocolate to 5 sq. (5 oz.) and butter to 5 tablespoons. Spread about 2 teaspoons chocolate mixture on flat side of each cookie.

Almond Wreaths

1 cup (5½ oz.) blanched almonds
2 cups sifted all-purpose flour
¾ cup butter
¼ cup sugar
1 egg, well beaten
Egg yolk, slightly beaten

1. Set out cookie sheets.
2. Finely chop almonds and set aside.
3. Measure flour and set aside.
4. Cream butter until softened.
5. Add sugar gradually, creaming until fluffy after each addition.
6. Blend in egg, in thirds.
7. Add the flour in fourths, blending well after each addition. Chill dough in refrigerator several hours.
8. Remove one-half the dough from refrigerator and turn onto a lightly floured surface. Roll ¼ in. thick. Cut rounds with a lightly floured 1¾-in. round cookie cutter. Using a lightly floured ¾-in. round cookie cutter, cut out centers of the cookies. Brush cookies lightly with egg yolk.
9. Sprinkle cookies with the chopped almonds. Carefully transfer to the cookie sheets.
10. Bake at 350°F 10 to 15 min.
11. With a spatula, carefully remove cookies to cooling rack.
12. Repeat above procedure for remainder of dough.

About 6 doz. cookies

Cinnamon Stars

2 cups (about ⅔ lb.) unblanched almonds (about 3½ cups, grated)
3 egg whites
1 cup confectioners' sugar
1 teaspoon grated lemon peel
¾ teaspoon cinnamon

1. Lightly grease two cookie sheets.
2. Grate almonds and set aside.
3. Beat egg whites until stiff peaks are formed.
4. Add sugar gradually, beating constantly.
5. Beat egg white-sugar mixture for 5 min. with an electric mixer on medium speed. Blend in lemon peel and cinnamon.
6. Set aside ½ cup of this meringue mixture and fold almonds into remaining meringue mixture. Gently pat or roll out 3/8 in. thick on canvas sprinkled with granulated sugar. Lightly sprinkle the top of the dough with more sugar. Cut out cookies with 2- to 2½-in. star-shaped cookie cutter dipped in confectioners' sugar. Carefully place stars on cookie sheets. Drop ½ teaspoon of the reserved meringue onto each cookie, drawing meringue out onto points of the star.
7. Bake at 325°F 15 to 18 min.
8. With a spatula, immediately remove cookies from cookie sheets to cooling racks.

About 3 doz. cookies

Anise Cookies

4½ cups sifted cake flour
1 teaspoon baking powder
4 eggs
3½ cups (1 lb.) sifted confectioners' sugar
4 teaspoons grated lemon peel
Anise seeds

1. Sift together and set aside flour and baking powder.
2. Beat eggs until thick and piled softly. (One-fourth teaspoon oil of anise added to the eggs at this time can be substituted for the anise seeds that are to be sprinkled on the cookie sheets.) Add gradually, beating until thoroughly mixed sugar and lemon peel.
3. Beat in dry ingredients in fourths, mixing thoroughly. Chill dough in refrigerator until firm enough to handle easily (about 1 hr.).
4. Lightly grease cookie sheets and sprinkle with anise seeds.
5. Roll dough ½ inch thick on lightly floured surface. Press lightly floured springerle rolling pin into dough, rolling carefully to make clear designs; or press mold down firmly. Brush surface gently with soft brush to remove excess flour. Cut cookies apart. With a spatula, gently lift them onto the cookie sheets. Cover with waxed paper and let them stand overnight.
6. Bake at 350°F 30 min., or until very slightly browned.
7. With a spatula, remove at once to cooling racks. When thoroughly cooled, store in a tightly covered jar for 1 or 2 weeks before using. (Storage period develops flavor and characteristic consistency. Cookies will keep for months.)

About 2½ doz. cookies

Peppernuts

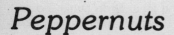

½ cup (2½ oz.) blanched almonds
4 cups sifted all-purpose flour
2 teaspoons cinnamon
½ teaspoon nutmeg
½ teaspoon allspice
½ teaspoon cloves
¼ teaspoon mace
¼ teaspoon salt
¼ teaspoon pepper
3 oz. candied citron (about ½ cup, chopped)
4 eggs
2 cups sugar
2¼ teaspoons brandy

1. Grease cookie sheets.
2. Grate almonds.
3. Sift together flour, cinnamon, nutmeg, allspice, cloves, mace, salt, and pepper into a bowl. Stir in the almonds and set aside.
4. Chop and set candied citron aside.
5. Beat eggs until thick and piled softly.
6. Add sugar gradually, beating thoroughly after each addition.
7. Add the flour-almond mixture in fourths, blending thoroughly after each addition. Mix in the citron. Turn about one-half the dough onto a lightly floured surface and roll ½ in. thick. Cut with a lightly floured 1-in. round cookie cutter. Transfer cookies to the cookie sheets.
8. Set out brandy.
9. Put a drop on the center of each cookie.
10. Bake at 350°F 15 to 20 min., or until cookies are lightly browned.
11. Remove to cooling racks, cool and store.

About 11 doz. cookies

Honey Cakes

3/4 cup (about 4 oz.) unblanched almonds
2 oz. candied orange peel (about 1/3 cup, chopped)
2 oz. candied lemon peel (about 1/3 cup;, chopped)
3 cups sifted all-purpose flour
1/4 teaspoon baking soda
1 teaspoon cinnamon
1/2 teaspoon allspice
1/2 teaspoon nutmeg
1/2 teaspoon cloves
2 eggs
1 cup sugar
1/2 cup honey
1/3 cup sifted confectioners' sugar
1 tablespoon water
1 teaspoon lemon juice

1. Grease a 15½x10½x1-in. pan.
2. Finely chop and set aside almonds, orange peel, and lemon peel.
3. Sift together flour, baking soda, cinnamon, allspice, nutmeg, and cloves and set aside.
4. Beat eggs and sugar until thick and piled softly.
5. Beat in honey. Gently fold in the dry ingredients in fourths. Mix in the almonds and candied peel. Turn batter into pan, spreading to corners.
6. Bake at 350°F 25 to 30 min., or until a wooden pick or cake tester comes out clean when inserted in center. Set pan on cooling rack.
7. Meanwhile, blend together confectioners' sugar, water, and lemon juice. When Lebkuchen is slightly cooled, spread mixture evenly over top and cut into 3x1½-in. bars. Remove to cooling rack.

About 2½ doz. cookies

Anise Drops

1½ cups sifted all-purpose flour
1/4 teaspoon baking powder
2 eggs
Water (enough to make 1/2 cup liquid)
1 cup sugar
1/4 teaspoon anise flavoring

1. Generously grease cookie sheets.
2. Sift together flour, and baking powder and set aside.
3. Put eggs into a liquid measuring cup.
4. Add water, if necessary.
5. Put into a mixing bowl with sugar and anise flavoring.
6. Beat until very thick and piled softly. Fold in the dry ingredients, sifting in about one-fourth at a time. Drop by teaspoonfuls onto the cookie sheets, about 2 in. apart. Set cookie sheets aside in a cool place (not in refrigerator) 8 to 10 hrs., or overnight. Do not cover cookies and do not disturb!
7. Bake at 350°F 5 to 6 min.
8. Remove to cooling racks to cool completely. Cookies form a cake-like layer on the bottom with a crisp "frosting" on the top.

About 4 doz. cookies

Index

German Index

English Index